PUERTO-RICAN
DISHES

PUERTO-RICAN DISHES

By

BERTA CABANILLAS, B.S., M.A.
Associate Professor
Home Economics Department
University of Puerto Rico

CARMEN GINORIO, B.S., M.A.
Associate Professor
Home Economics Department
University of Puerto Rico

**EDITORIAL DE LA
UNIVERSIDAD DE PUERTO RICO**

Authors' edition: 1956, 1966, 1972
Fourth Edition: 1974
Reprints: 1977, 1984, 1990, 1993, 1998, 2000, 2001, 2002

Catalogación de la Biblioteca del Congreso
Library of Congress Cataloging-in-Publication Data

Cabanillas de Rodríguez, Berta. 1894-1974
    Puerto Rican Dishes / by Berta Cabanillas, Carmen Ginorio.
    p. cm.
    Reprint. Originally published: 4th Ed. 1974
    ISBN -8477-2780-7
    1. Cookery, Puerto Rican   I. Ginorio, Carmen.   II. Title.
TX716.P8C33   1990
641.597295--dc20

IMPRESO EN LOS ESTADOS UNIDOS DE AMÉRICA
PRINTED IN THE UNITED STATES OF AMERICA

Editorial de la Universidad de Puerto Rico
PO Box 23322
San Juan, Puerto Rico 00931-3322
Administración: Tel. (809) 250-0000 / Fax (809) 753-9116
Depto. Ventas: Tel. (809) 758-8345 / Fax (809) 751-8785

CONTENTS

[v]

PREFACE

We are publishing this book because we consider it our duty as Puerto-Ricans to make available in English the recipes we have inherited from our ancestors. They are associated in our memories with the "fiestas" of our happy childhood days and to the ritual of our food customs and traditions as observed in our homes; therefore, we want to share with others the pleasures derived from the dishes we enjoy so much.

We have always felt the need of a recipe book in English for the large group of North Americans living among us, so that they can make the best use of the different vegetables, fruits, and other food materials new to them. Thus, at the request of many of our American friends, we decided to write this book.

When we study the origin of our dishes and our food habits we find they have a very close relation with the development of agriculture and with other factors such as exchange of products among countries and regions and transportation facilities.

We are indebted to the Borinquen indians for their contribution in raising of corn, yuca, sweet potatoes, pineapple, leren, peanuts, etc.; to Columbus, who brought in his ships seeds of all sorts: rice, fruits, vegetables; to the Spanish colonizers, who brought from the Mother Country their food customs and the dishes they loved so much, like "cocido", "gazpacho", "bacalao a la Vizcaina", and others.

King Ferdinand had a great interest in the development of agriculture in the colony and he ordered, by royal decree, in 1511, the establishment of an experimental farm[1] in the Toa River valley for the introduction of new plants and for the adoption of new methods in agriculture, in order to increase the food supply of the new colony. The Spanish missionaries cultivated orchards and also raised new plants brought in by them.[2] Even to the boats bringing slaves from Guinea and the Gold Coast in Africa we are grateful for bringing us the yam and the banana.

(1) This is the first experiment station in the New World.
(2) Father Tomás de Berlanga introduced the plantain in 1516 and Father Diego Lorenzo the cocoanut palm, besides the guinea hen in 1549.

[vii]

In this short historical summary of our foods only an incomplete account can be given, but we may add that the location of Puerto Rico among a chain of islands, between two continents made possible a continuous dispersion route óf plants and seeds from Central and South America. It made possible for the avocado, the papaya, the squash, cacao, the níspero, the apio, the potato, some beans, and yautías to become part of our flora.

We have included in this book those recipes which we .consider representative of our cookery. In this important task, two friends proved of great help by selecting them. There are some recipes which should be included, so they are given in Chapter XI, and a few menus which may be helpful to the housewife. A glossary is given at the end of the book to help understand many names and words we have given in Spanish, for lack of an adequate translation into the English.

We wish to acknowledge our indebtedness to several friends who have helped with their constructive criticisms, suggestions and encouragement in the preparation of this book. We wish especially to express our appreciation to Dr. Lydia J. Roberts and Mrs. Doris M. Cabanillas for the selection of recipes, to Mrs. Lucille K. Ramírez who helped us in the translation of recipes for chapters four and five, Mrs. Marion W. Cumpiano and Miss Cecil E. Stevens for reading and correcting the manuscript, to Miss Carmen Gómez Tejera and Miss Lydia E. Huber for their valuable suggestions and to Mr. Pedro Osuna and Mr. Teodoro Soto of Extension Service for reading and checking the lists on fruits and vegetables. To all of them we tender our grateful thanks.

BERTA CABANILLAS
CARMEN GINORIO

December 1955
University of Puerto Rico

CHAPTER I

STEP INTO THE KITCHEN

Kitchen arrangement

We step into the kitchen to start work and prepare one of our favorite recipes. The success of the job does not depend exclusively on the quality of food materials we use, nor the exactness of the recipe, but on the organization of the work, the location of the kitchen equipment into working areas, and the arrangement and accessibility of utensils.

If the kitchen is not conveniently arranged into working areas, much time and energy is wasted, going around from stove to sink, from refrigerator to cupboards, looking for utensils or materials. The equipment and utensils should be grouped according to their use at three work areas: food preparation, cooking and cleaning area. The food preparation area is where all the preliminary work for cooking is done: peeling, slicing, grinding, etc. The refrigerator is at this center. It is necessary to have counter space to work, either a cabinet or a table; and located in this section all the necessary utensils to carry on these tasks.

Near the sink, cupboards or shelves are indispensable at the cleaning center, also the utensils and cleansing supplies necessary for dishwashing. In the cooking area the stove should be conveniently located in relation to other areas. There should be ample space across the kitchen, between pieces of equipment, so two persons can work at a time without bumping or interfering with each other.

Yesterday and today

The description given in the preceding paragraph is that of the modern kitchen. Gone are the days of the "fogón" and the "anafre" as the standard type of stove for food preparation in most of the Puerto Rican homes. The "fogón" is a built-in stove, made either of cement, bricks or tiles. It is like a rectangular box, with three to five grates on top (hornillas) and all along from one. end to another of the

[1]

"fogón" and under the grates there is an open space to receive the ashes with openings at both ends. Under the fogón there is a recessed space to keep charcoal needed in boxes or bags. The "anafre" is a kind of brazier, made of cast iron, purchased at any store. The "anafre" has only one grate and is movable, and can be placed on a table or bench, or even on a strong sand box.

Until the beginning of this century the elegant homes of the well-to-do families had the most attractive "fogón" made of very decorative Spanish tiles, and in many homes, a hood was built over them to collect smoke and carry it out through a small chimney. Of course, these kitchens were quite large, and working in them meant 'much energy spent going around and many tired cook or housewife at the end of the days' work. But the kitchen today is smaller, scientifically planned, and better arranged. As it is difficult to get help and more time is needed for social and civic activities, the housewife must plan her work very carefully.

The social changes have also affected our cookery; the housewife, besides being the cook, is also the gracious hostess, the devoted mother and wife, and a civic leader. As a result cookery is simpler and meals are less elaborate.

Kitchen utensils

Among all the modern utensils needed in the kitchen for preparing the recipes given in this book, there are several pieces which are "traditional" in the Puerto Rican home and which, in our opinion, can not be replaced by any modern device: these humble utensils are: the grater (rallo) and the mortar and pestle (pilón y maceta). For all the dishes prepared from cocoanuts, the grater renders excellent service in producing a finely shredded cocoanut from which is easier to extract the "milk", or for preparing "dulce de coco", "arroz con coco".

In seasoning poultry, meat, and the suckling pig for "lechón asado" as well as other foods, the mortar grinds and combines so well the orégano, garlic, salt, culinary herbs and other seasonings for "rubbing" meats that they have a better flavor, when seasoning is "rubbed" over the surface.

For preparing boiled rice, a "caldero" is most adequate. Do not attempt to make any kind of rice in a saucepan or any utensil with thin bottom and sides. The next best substitute for the "caldero" is a Dutch oven. For preparing legumes, such as "habichuelas guisadas" an aluminum kettle, straight sides and flat bottom with cover is best.

Measuring

To succeed in food preparation the use of standard measuring equipment is of utmost importance. Accurate measurements are essential. Every kitchen should be equipped with a set of standard measuring cups as well as a set of standard measuring spoons. The standard cup is one-half pint and is divided into quarts and thirds. They are made of aluminum, tin, glass or plastic material.

For dry ingredients use measuring cups with 1 cup line at the rim or a set of 4 measuring cups of a ¼ cup, ⅓ cup, ½ cup and a 1 cup measure. For liquid ingredients use measuring cups with the rim above the 1 cup line to avoid spilling.

Sets of measuring spoons consist of a ¼ teaspoon, ½ teaspoon, 1 teaspoon and a 1 tablespoon, they come attached to a ring.

EQUIVALENT MEASUREMENTS

60 drops	1 teaspoon
3 teaspoons	1 tablespoon
16 tablespoons	1 cup
2 cups	1 pint
2 pints	1 quart
4 quarts	1 gallon
1 ounce	28.4 grams
16 ounces	1 pound
1 pound	454 grams
1 kilo	2 lbs. 2⅗ ounces

Measuring hints

If you measure the dry ingredients before measuring the liquid ones, you do less washing by using the same cup for both purposes.

Sift flour before measuring and do not shake down.

It is convenient to have in the kitchen a 2-cups measure or a 1-quart measure to save time when preparing food in large quantities for special occasions.

Pack down brown sugar as it is measured.

Less than ¼ cup should be measured by spoonfuls.

Solid fats are easily measured by placing cold water in the measuring cup and leaving a space equal to the amount of fat to be measured, then drain off the water.

[3]

The following tables on weights and equivalents will be useful in calculating the food materials needed and the cost of recipes.

NUMBER OF TEASPOONS IN 1 OUNCE OF SPICES AND OTHER FOODS

Baking powder	8	teaspoons
Butter	6	"
Cinnamon	14	"
Cloves	12	"
Cornstarch	9	"
Flour	12	"
Gelatine	12	"
Ginger	15	"
Lemon juice	6	"
Mayonnaise	6	"
Mustard	14	"
Nutmeg	11	"
Olive oil	7½	"
Pepper	11	"
Salt	6	"
Soda	2½	"
Sugar	6	"
Vanilla extract	8	"

APPROXIMATE WEIGHT OF 1 CUP OF SOME FOODS

Bread crumbs	5	ounces
Cornflakes	½	"
Corn syrup	10	"
Corn starch	5⅛	"
Cream of wheat	6	"
Evaporated milk (undiluted)	9	"
Honey	11	"
Molasses	12	"
Oatmeal	3⅛	"
Olive Oil	7½	"
Sesame Seed	5	"

EQUIVALENT AMOUNTS

Food	Weight	Approximate Measure
Apio (arracacha), grated	1 lb.	¾ cup
Bananas, diced	1 lb. (3 medium)	2½ cups
Beans, kidneys, uncooked	1 lb.	2½ cups
Beef, ground	1 lb.	2 cups
Butter	1 lb.	2 cups
Butter, bar	¼ lb.	½ cup

EQUIVALENT AMOUNTS (*Continued*)

Food	*Weight*	*Approximate Measure*
Cheese, American, grated	1 lb.	4 cups
Cheese, Parmesan, grated	1 lb.	5 cups
Cheese, cream, pkg.	3 ozs.	6 tbsp.
Chick peas, uncooked	1 lb.	2 cups
Chocolate, grated	1 lb.	3 cups
Cocoa	1 lb.	4 cups
Cocoanut, large	1½ lbs.	3 cups
Coffee, ground fine	1 lb.	5–6 cups
Cornmeal	1 lb.	3 cups
Corn starch	1 lb.	3 cups
Dates, pitted, pkg.	7¼ ozs.	1¼ cups
Eggplant, boiled, mashed	1 lb.	1¾ cups
Egg, whites	8–10	1 cup
Fish, boiled, flaked	1 lb.	2 cups
Flour	1 lb.	4 cups
Ginger ale	1–13 fl. ozs.	1½ cups
Guavas, diced	1 lb.	1 cup
Lemon, juice	1 medium	1 tbsp.
Mangoes, diced	3–4	2 cups
Margarine	1 lb.	2 cups
Milk, dry	1 lb.	4 cups
Milk, evaporated	14½ ozs. can	1⅔ cups
Milk, evaporated	6 ozs. can	¾ cup
Milk, sweetened, condensed	14 ozs. can	1¼ cups
Nuts, cut	1 lb.	4 cups
Onion, diced	1 lb.	2–3 cups
Orange, juice	4 medium	1 cup
Pigeon peas	1 lb.	2⅔ cups
Potatoes, boiled, mashed	1 lb.	2 cups
Prunes, dried, stoned	1 lb.	2 cups
Pumpkin, boiled, mashed	1 lb.	1¼ cups
Raisin, seedless	15 ozs. pkg.	3 cups
Rice	1 lb.	2⅛ cups
Rice, cooked	1 lb.	3–4 cups
Rice, meal	1 lb.	2⅔ cups
Soda water	12 fl. ozs.	1½ cups
Sugar, granulated	1 lb.	2¼ cups
Sugar, powdered	1 lb.	3½ cups
Sugar, brown	1 lb.	2⅔ cups
Sweet potatoes, boiled, mashed	1 lb.	1⅓ cups
Yautia, grated	1 lb.	1¼ cups
Yautia, boiled, mashed	1 lb.	1¼ cups
Yolks	12 yolks	1 cup
Yuca, grated	1 lb.	1¼ cups

Cooking hints

Use a wooden spoon to stir hot mixtures as the metal spoon heats too quickly.

Use a rubber spatula for scraping.

To cream butter easily scald the bowl before using.

Keep a small pan with perforated lid for preparing achote coloring, then strain into a glass container; cover and place in refrigerator for future use.

To soften dry bread, sprinkle with water and heat in the oven for few minutes.

Fat should be preheated a little more than the correct cooking temperature as it cools when cold food is put into it.

A tablespoon of fat in the water for cooking macaroni or similar products will prevent them from sticking.

To keep parsley or other seasoning herbs fresh put them in a covered jar in the refrigerator.

Use sharp kitchen scissors to cut lettuce leaves, parsley, cabbage, and stems from water cress, also to dice chicken for chicken salad.

When making Cornmeal Turnover or Alcapurria, shape them on a piece of greased plantain leaf, waxed paper or a small plate and they will slip easily into the frying pan.

If plantain leaves are not available for wrapping pasteles use parchment paper.

If you do not have enough plantain leaves, wrap the pasteles first in a piece of plantain leaf and then in a piece of parchment paper.

Arrange oven racks and preheat oven 10 to 15 minutes.

If only one pan is to be used place it in the center of the rack. If two or more pans are used do not place one under the other, arrange them diagonally so heat can circulate. Never overload the oven.

Do not open door too frequently.

If lemons are allowed to stand in hot water for five minutes, they are easier to squeeze and they will yield more juice.

When peeling oranges or grapefruits place them in boiling water and let stand for five minutes. The inner white peeling will come off easily.

To extract most of the "milk" from cocoanut and sesame seeds, hot water is added to the grated cocoanut or ground seeds.

To ripen green bananas, wrap in paper and keep in a dark place.

To prevent ripening of breadfruit keep in water overnight, or in the refrigerator.

Lemon or orange juice sprinkled over bananas or alligator pears will prevent them from turning dark.

Place almonds in boiling water for few minutes and the skin will peel off easily.

To make tough meats tender, wrap in papaya leaves, or cover with slices of green papaya.

When preparing beef stew with a less tender cut, use green papaya instead of potatoes.

Always place soup meat in cold water for a few minutes before cooking so that all the juices of the meat will be extracted.

Always buy freshly roasted and ground coffee and do not keep it too long. After opening a bag of coffee, keep it in a covered container.

Peeling a green plantain or banana needs some explanation. Make a lengthwise slit, skin deep and then remove skin with a pointed knife or thumb. To prevent staining your hands: a) Rub hands with fat or lemon juice. b) Peel plantain under water.

Place peeled green plantain or banana in salted water to prevent them from turning dark.

The stain of plantain and genip are very difficult to remove from fabrics. Use care when working with them.

CHAPTER II

FRUITS

Guavas, pineapple, soursop, cocoplum and other fruits grew wild in the island and were used by the Indians when Ponce de León began the colonization of Puerto Rico. Since then, the Spanish conquerors brought more fruits and food plants from Spain and other regions: papaya from Central America, guinep from Venezuela, Otaheite gooseberry from the Orient, tamarind and mangoes from India, bananas from Africa and citrus fruits and pomegranate from Spain.

Our fruits are rich sources of vitamin A and C, guavas, papaya, oranges, lemons and especially the West Indian cherry (cereza, acerola) recently discovered as the richest source of Vitamin C.[1]

With an abundance of sugar and fruits, these food materials have been combined from the earliest times to prepare such characteristic desserts as fruit preserves: "dulces en almíbar", jellies, pastes and candied fruits. One of the early historians was so surprised by the immense amounts of "dulces" consumed in the Indies (new world) he stated that it was incredible.[2]

Very nice sherbets and ices are also prepared from our fruits. Other frozen dessert is the "mantecado" or French ice cream, using milk and egg yolks as a base and adding fruit pulp or other flavoring as cocoanut, almond or coffee.

Fruits may be found at the market the year round. For some of them the season is quite short, two or three months but, few as papaya, bananas and cocoanuts are found the whole year. Following is a list of the most common fruits:

BANANA. Guineo; musa sapientum. Found at the markets the year round; used as a food staple when green, as a dessert fruit when ripe. There are the following varieties:

   Lady's finger or fig banana; guineo niño, de piña, de rosa, dátil;

---

[1] Two cherries are enough to supply the daily requirement of vitamin C. (70 mg.)

Cobos, Bernabe P., Historia del Nuevo Mundo, II, p. 409.

it is the smallest banana, with a thin peel, and has a sweet, delicate flavor.

Apple banana; guineo manzano. Next in size to the fig banana. It has a fine flavor, slightly acid resembling apple flavor.

Giant banana; guineo gigante o guarán; largest of all bananas, triangular pointed.

Monte Cristo; a form of the giant banana, shorter and round, round end, fruit is greener, most common.

Morado; largest and cheapest of the bananas; reddish or brownish purple fruit; poor flavor, should be cooked for consumption.

CASHEW NUT. Pajuil, cajuil; anacardim occidentale. Common tree near the seashore, especially near Vega Baja; fruits are either red or yellow color or both; the juice is astringent, fruit is made into preserves or candied and the nut is roasted.

CITRON. Cidra; citrus medica. Grows in the mountains's coffee section; used for preserves and candied. Not common at the markets.

COCONUT. Coco; cocos nucifera. Cocoanut water is obtained from the green cocoanut, pulp is soft. The pulp of the dried fruit is hard; it is grated and by adding water the "milk" is extracted. Very rich in oil.

COCOPLUM. Hicaco: chrysobalanus icaco. Never cultivated nor marketed, grows along the coast; large seed, thin pulp, fruit varies in color, white, or pale pinkish or purplish black. Used for preserves.

CUSTARD APPLE. Corazón; annona reticulata. Pinky or rosy pulp, very sweet; soft to the touch when ripe.

GENIPAP. Jagua; genipa americana. Strong flavor and odor; used for the preparation of a tonic drink. Fruit has a light brownish color, about the size of a large orange.

GRAPEFRUIT. Toronja; citrus medica. The best varieties are the Marsh seedless and the Duncan which has more seeds. The Marsh variety is sweeter and the fruit is not round as the Duncan.

GUAMA. Inga laurina. Green pods, white, sweet juicy pulp surrounding the seeds.

GUAVA. Guayaba; psidium guajava. There are several varieties differing in size, color and flavor: small, large, pear shaped; yellow, pink or reddish pulp; sweet or very acid. Best fruit for jelly; and also for preserves, drinks and sherbets.

GUINEP. Quenepa; melicocca bijuga. Abundant in the south, in Ponce;

[9]

small fruit, green skin, large seed with a thin layer of acid pulp. Astringent if fruit is not ripe.

HEVI. Jobo de la India; spondias dulcis. Yellow thin skin, acid pulp, large spiny seed.

LIME. Limón agrio; citrus aurantifolia. Most common, small fruit, good flavor.

LIME (SWEET). Limón dulce; citrus limetta. Not very common; fruit as large as the orange, smooth thin, lime green skin.

MANGO. Mango; mangifera indica. The most common tree fruit in the island, there are several varieties; the "blanco" or white is found in the western part of the island at Mayagüez, the large, fibrous variety; the piña (pineapple) and the fiberless variety. Large seed, sweet, rich pulp used for pastes and preserves; when medium ripe are used also for pies.

ORANGE. China; naranja dulce; citrus sinensis. There are several varieties: among them the "Nebo" (Washington navel) seedless and Valencia.

ORANGE (SOUR). Naranja agria; citrus aurantium. Grows wild, "dulces" made from the inner white peeling.

OTAHEITE GOOSEBERRY. Grosella; cicca disticha. Small yellow fruit, very acid juicy pulp surrounding a small seed. When cooked into preserves becomes a bright red.

PAPAYA. Lechosa; carica papaya. The most useful fruit, when ripe may be eaten as a melon, is used for sherbets; when green is eaten as a vegetable and used for preserves. The leaves, unripe fruit and trunk contain a milky substance rich in papain. Delicate flavor, sweet, soft, yellow or deep pink flesh.

PINEAPPLE. Piña; ananas ananas. The Red Spanish variety is small and the Smooth Cayenne is medium size; the Cabezona is the largest in size but it is not so common as the other two. The Red Spanish and the Smooth Cayenne are sometimes sold at the roadside markets.

POMEGRANATE. Granada; punica granatum. Yellowish thick skin, several small seeds surrounded by pink, juicy pulp; used for drinks; sweet, low acidity.

ROSEAPPLE. Pomarrosa; eugenia jambos. Has a fine rose perfume, not very sweet, eaten fresh, used for preserves.

SAPODILLA. Níspero; sapota achras. Excellent fruit, but not very abundant. Small, reddish-brown skin; pulp has a smooth texture and delicate flavor. Eaten out-of-hand or cut in halves and eaten with a spoon.

SEA GRAPE. Uva de playa; coccolobis uvifera. Grows wild along the seashore, seldom found at the markets. Large seed and little flesh, varies from sweet to acid; purple or white fruits.

SOURSOP. Guanábana; annona muricata. Large fruit with curved spines; sweet, white, juicy pulp; eaten fresh and used for drinks and sherbets. There are two varieties: the sweet and the acid.

STAR APPLE. Caimito; chrysophyllum caimito. Fruits are of two colors either purple (almost black) or green.

SUGAR APPLE. Anón; annona squamosa. Resembles the custard apple, but has a yellowish-green rind, made up of segments; soft pulp. Dessert fruit.

TAMARIND. Tamarindo; tamarindus indica. Pod with black seeds surrounded with pulp, very acid. Used for drinks.

TROPICAL ALMOND. Almendra; terminalia catappa. Small nut surrounded by pulp, resembles the true almond.

WEST INDIAN CHERRY. Cereza colorada; malpighia puniciflora. Small red fruit, three spongy seeds; very acid, eaten fresh or cooked in preserves and other desserts.

WEST INDIAN LOCUST. Algarroba; hymenaea courbaril. Large, hard shell pod with seeds covered with flowry aril enclosed in a large hard shell pod. Edible but has a very disagreeable odor.

YELLOW MOMBIN. Ciruela amarilla; spondias mombin. Small fruit, large seed, soft juicy flesh, sweet, slightly acid.[3]

Preparation of Fresh Fruits

Fresh fruits are always tempting and agreeable either as appetizers or as part of the menu. Most of the fruits may be served as appetizer or in easily made desserts. Some simple ways of serving fresh fruits are:

Oranges and grapefruits:

1. Cut in halves. With a sharp paring knife cut around the sections or "gajos" to loosen from the dividing membrane. For decoration the edge may be cut indented.

2. Cut off each end of fruit. Remove yellow and inner white peeling

---

[3] There is a wild true jobillo (spondias ciruoella) which resembles the yellow mombin; the fruit is sweeter and larger, but is not edible.

at the same time. Arrange in a plate like the petals of a flower. Garnish with red cherries in the center or a mound of powdered sugar.

3. Cut yellow peeling and shape as a basket. Remove "gajos" or pulp and cut in pieces. Mix with diced bananas and pineapple or other fruits. Refill basket and garnish with lemon leaves.

4. Serve whole fruit by removing the yellow and white peeling at the same time. The sections may be easily removed and eaten with a fork.

5. Peel the yellow rind thinly with a knife and remove one end and suck (native style).

6. Squeeze juice, remove only seeds but leave pulp. Serve very cold.

Fruit juices should be squeezed just before serving. If it is prepared ahead of time, it may be kept in a glass or china container well covered. When squeezing the juice, remove the rind from the middle, just where it is cut in halves, to prevent the bitter oil of the rind from getting into the juice.

Pineapple

1. Peel pineapple and cut in slices. Remove hard core in center and garnish with native cherries.

2. Peel pineapple and cut in cubes. Take best leaves from "crown" and arrange around fruit plate or sherbet glass. Place some crushed ice in bottom and pineapple cubes on top. Sprinkle with sugar and garnish with native cherry.

3. Cut pineapple in halves, lengthwise from crown to stem. Remove pulp and cut in cubes. Refill shell and garnish with cherries and papaya balls. See illustration.

4. Cut around each "tuft" or natural section with a sharp pointed knife. Remove each tuft separately and arrange in a plate. Place in the center a mound or cone of powdered sugar. The pointed end or pulp should be toward the center and peel will then be toward the outside.

Papaya

1. Chill and serve in slices, like melon. Garnish with lemon slices or quarters.

2. Scoop out balls with ball cutter and serve in cocktail glasses, chill before serving. Garnish with native cherries.

3. Mash pulp, add lemon juice, sugar, water and crushed ice. Serve as a cold drink.

[12]

Bananas[4]

1. Used in fruit cocktail.

Mango and hevi

Remove peel and serve whole. Pulp may be sliced[5] and eaten with fork or hold with fork and "sucked". There is no pleasure like holding a mango in your hands and peel as you eat even though your face and hands get sticky. Someone has recommended a bathtub as the best place to eat mango that way.

Guavas

1. Remove both ends and cut in eighths. Arrange sections like petals of a flower.
2. Serve whole to be cut and eaten with fork.
3. Cut in cubes and serve with sugar, milk or cream.

Star apple and níspero

1. Cut in halves and serve very cold; pulp may be eaten with a teaspoon.
2. Níspero may also be cut in quarters and eaten with a fork.

Soursop and custard apple

1. May be cut in sections and eaten with a spoon.
2. The seeds may be removed, add few drops of lemon juice and eaten with a spoon.

Fruit cocktail

Most of the fruits can be served as fruit cocktail. There are many possible combinations such as:
        a. Oranges, bananas, and grapefruits
        b. Pineapple, papaya and mango
        c. Banana, grapefruit and pineapple
        d. Mango, bananas and oranges
        e. Papaya, grapefruit, and banana
Fruits are cut in small pieces and mixed carefully. Half a teaspoon

---

[4] Ripe bananas are prepared to accompany other dishes.
[5] Mangoes are sliced away from the stem parallel to the flat sides of the stone.

[13]

of lemon juice added will improve the flavor and prevent the bananas for turning dark. To garnish use a native cherry or a piece of guava jelly. Serve very cold as appetizer or dessert. See illustration.

AMBROSIA 4 servings

4 oranges	1 cup grated cocoanut
4 bananas	Sugar

Peel orange and remove sections and cut in small pieces. Peel and cut banana, making two cuts lengthwise at right angles, slice then in cubes. Mix fruits carefully with fork, add cocoanut and sugar. Serve very cold and garnish with a native cherry or papaya balls.

Fruit preserves

The most typical way to prepare the fruits is by cooking them in a heavy syrup. This is known as "dulces en almíbar". When there is abundance of papayas, sour oranges, guavas, etc., they are prepared and placed in well covered glass or china containers for future use. If kept in the refrigerator they will last for several months. "Dulce de coco" because of its fat content can not stand as long as other "dulces" made from fruits.

PAPAYA PRESERVE 8–10 servings

1–2 pounds green papaya	Sugar
4 sticks cinnamon	

Peel papaya and slice into pieces about 3 inches long and ½ inch thick. Boil until papaya is slightly cooked. Remove from water and measure. For each cup of cooked papaya use ½ cup water in which the papaya was boiled and ½ cup sugar. Boil sugar and water then add the papaya and cinnamon. Cook slowly until papaya is transparent and the syrup is thick.

SOUR ORANGE PRESERVE 8–10 servings

6 sour oranges	Sugar

Wash oranges, peel yellow rind very thin. Cut through the peel and remove in four sections. Place in hot water for 8 to 10 hours and change it as soon as it turns yellow. Boil white peel until tender.

Measure peel by cups and add the same proportion of water and sugar as for Papaya Preserve. Cook until peel is clear and syrup is thick.

TOMATO PRESERVE
10–12 servings

2 pounds tomatoes
1 quart water

1 pound sugar
4 sticks cinnamon

Blanch tomatoes for five minutes. Remove from water and peel. Measure one quart of the water in which the tomatoes were blanched, add the sugar and cinnamon and boil for few minutes. Add the tomatoes and cook until syrup is thick.

COCOANUT PRESERVE
6–8 servings

1 grated cocoanut
Sugar

Lemon peel

Measure cocoanut and for each cup of cocoanut add ½ cup water and boil for few minutes. Measure again and for each cup of cocoanut add ¾ cups sugar, lemon peel and cook at a low heat until syrup is thick.

GUAVA SHELLS PRESERVE
6–8 servings

1 pound guavas
2 pounds sugar

2 cups water

Peel guavas very thin. Cut in halves and remove seeds. Cook shells until they are slightly tender, remove from water and drain. Add sugar to the water in which guava shells were cooked. Boil for a few minutes and then add the shells. Cook slowly. When syrup is thick remove from heat.

Jellies, Pastes and Marmalades

For jelly making the fruit must contain pectin and acid. Guava is the fruit containing both in suitable amounts. Other fruits contain pectin but in smaller amounts and it is difficult to obtain a firm jelly. Guavas should not be ripe but "pintonas", that is, just beginning to ripen, when they have the greatest amount of pectin.

Oranges and grapefruits also have pectin in the inner white peel. To know if a fruit contains pectin, it is cut in pieces and boiled. Strain

[15]

water and to 1 teaspoon add 2 teaspoons of alcohol. If pectin is present, a gelatine will be formed as thick as egg white. If a thinner gelatine develops, the amount of pectin is not sufficient for jelly making.

Pastes are made from the pulp of some fruits as guavas, mangoes, inner white peel of sour oranges and grapefruit, pineapples, etc. Pastes and marmalades should be cooked at low heat to prevent the caramelization of sugar.

In candying soft-pulp fruits such as papaya, it may be necessary to place them in the sunshine to dry and roll in sugar several times. If day is damp fruit will not dry. Never attempt to candy fruits during rainy days.

GUAVA JELLY

3 pound guavas   Sugar

Wash guavas, remove both ends and cut in quarters. Place in a flat bottomed pan and add enough water to cover guavas. Boil until guavas are tender. Strain in a jelly bag but do not squeeze. Measure the juice and for each cup add a cup of sugar. Stir to dissolve sugar. Boil rapidly. The jelly test is when the spoon is dipped into the syrup and when lifted allow the syrup to drop back into the pan, and the last two drops fall from the spoon at once. If a thermometer is used it will register a temperature of 220° to 224°F. Pour at once in a sterilized jar. Remove scum and cover with melted paraffin. See illustration.

GUAVA PASTE

4 pounds guavas   Sugar

Wash guavas, remove both ends and cut in quarters. Place in saucepan, cover with water and cook until guavas are tender. Remove from water, mash and strain. Measure the pulp and for each cup use 1½ cups sugar. Place in kettle and cook slowly, stirring constantly. When mixture separates from sides of pan paste is done. Pour into a shallow pan, or tray. Bottom and sides of pan should be damp to prevent paste from sticking. See illustration.

SOUR ORANGE PASTE

6 sour oranges   Sugar

Wash oranges, peel yellow rind very thinly. Cut through the peel

[16]

and remove the white inner peel in 4 sections. Place in hot water for 8 or 10 hours, changing water frequently while it turns into a yellowish color. Boil white peel until tender. Grind peel and measure. To each cup of ground peel add 1 cup sugar. Place in pan and mix well. Cook slowly, stirring constantly. When mixture separates from sides of pan, paste is done. Pour into a shallow pan or tray. Dip a knife in water and run over paste to make surface smooth. Place in sunshine to dry.

MANGO PASTE

Wash, peel and slice mangoes. Mash pulp and strain. Measure pulp and add equal amounts of sugar. Cook slowly stirring constantly until mixture separates from sides of pan. Pour in a shallow rectangular pan and let dry.

Native Cherry Paste

Hevi Paste

Follow directions for Mango Paste.

Orange Marmalade   2 cups

    4 oranges   Sugar

Wash oranges and grate yellow rind slightly to open pores so oil is removed. Place in hot water and change water frequently. Slice oranges very thin, including rind and pulp. Remove any seeds and white fiber between sections. Measure pulp and add 3 cups water for each cup of pulp. Cook at low heat until rind is tender and clear. Measure again, and for each cup of pulp and liquid add ¾ cups sugar. Cook slowly. When syrup is thick and two drops fall from side of spoon pour in sterilized jars. When cool, cover and put away.

GRAPEFRUIT MARMALADE

Follow directions for Orange Marmalade.

TROPICAL MARMALADE   1 quart jar

    1–3 pounds pineapple   3 oranges
    2 lemons   Sugar

Slice lemons and oranges and cook as for Orange Marmalade. Grate

[17]

pineapple and add to oranges. Measure and for each cup of pulp add
¾ cup sugar. Cook slowly and when syrup is thick and rind clear
pour into jars.

GUAVA MARMALADE

Follow directions for Guava Paste but remove from heat before paste
is firm.

PINEAPPLE MARMALADE   2 cups

   1–3 pounds pineapple   Sugar

Grate pineapple. Measure and for each cup of pulp add ¾ cup sugar.
Cook slowly, and remove from heat when syrup is thick.

CANDIED GRAPEFRUIT PEEL   32 slices

   4 grapefruits   Sugar

Grate grapefruit slightly to remove yellow rind. Cut through the peel
and remove white inner peel into four sections, then cut each section
into two or four strips, or more if desired. Place in hot water and
change water as often as it turns yellowish. Place grapefruit peel in
water and cook until tender. Remove from heat, drain off water and
measure. For each cup of peel add 3 cups water and 3 cups sugar.
Place peel in saucepan and add all the water and one third of the
sugar and boil for 30 minutes. Add another third of the sugar and
boil again for 30 minutes. Add the rest of the sugar and cook slowly.
When peel is clear and syrup very thick remove from heat. Drain the
strips very well and roll in granulated sugar. If necessary place in the
sunshine to dry.

CANDIED CITRON
CANDIED ORANGE PEEL

Follow directions for Candied Grapefruit Peel.

CANDIED CASHEW NUT   9 servings

   18 cashew nuts   6 cups sugar
   6 cups water

Discard nut, place fruit in water and boil until tender. Remove from
water and drain. Place fruit in water, add 2 cups sugar and boil for

[18]

30 minutes. Add 2 more cups of sugar and boil for another 30 minutes. Add 2 more cups of sugar and cook slowly for 30 minutes. When syrup gets very thick remove fruits and drain very well. Roll in granulated sugar and let dry. If necessary place fruits in the sunshine; roll them in sugar several times, turning them over, so they will dry well.

CANDIED PINEAPPLE

CANDIED PAPAYA

It is not necessary to boil fruit before candying as the pulp of the pineapple and papaya is rather soft. The pulp have more water than grapefruit or orange peel, the syrup must be more concentrated. Use the proportion of 2 cups water and 3 cups sugar for each cup of pineapple or papaya pulp. Follow directions for Candied Grapefruit Peel.

Fruit Ices and Ice Cream

Among the most popular desserts are fruit ices and ice creams. They are appetizing, refreshing and nourishing; and as desserts they increase the food value of any meal.

Delicious ices can be prepared from most of our fruits, having fruit juices or fruit pulp as the basic ingredients. Ice creams with custard or milk as a foundation are also flavored with fruit juice or fruit pulp.

To freeze ice cream about 20 pounds of ice are needed for $1\frac{1}{2}$ quarts of ice cream mixture. Ice is crushed to sizes not larger than a native almond. The salt used is a coarse salt, sold by the pound. The proportion is 1 part salt to 6 or 8 parts of ice.

The ice cream mixture is poured into the inner metal container filled to about $\frac{2}{3}$ of its capacity and is placed into the wooden can. All the ice should be crushed at once and mixed with the salt in the correct proportion.

A layer of crushed ice about 2 inches deep is put first, and then the mixture of ice and salt may be added. Ice should be packed well. Adjust the lid and crank well and keep the lid tight. For the first 7 minutes turn the crank slowly, so all the mixture is cooled uniformly. After that time turn the crank faster until it becomes quite heavy and difficult to turn. It is then frozen and ready to serve.

Good care should be taken of the freezer, rinse the inner metal can in hot water and dry well then rinse the outer wooden can and turn it up-side down to dry. Wipe the lid and crank with a damp cloth and remove all particles of salt. When all parts are dried, assemble together and put away.

ALMOND ICE CREAM   15 servings

Prepare the recipe for Ice Cream, omit vanilla and add ¼ pound ground almonds and 1 teaspoon almond extract. Freeze.

BANANA ICE CREAM   15 servings

2 cups banana pulp	2 cups milk
1 cup orange juice	1¼ cups sugar

Add orange juice to pulp and let stand in refrigerator for ½ hour. Strain. Add sugar and milk. Freeze.

NATIVE CHERRY ICE   15 servings

2 pounds cherries	3 cups water
2 pounds sugar	

Wash the cherries and remove seeds. Rinse seeds with water to remove any juice of pulp left, then add the water to the pulp and strain. Add sugar and freeze.

COCOANUT ICE   20 servings

2 cocoanuts	1½ cups sugar
6 cups hot water	1 teaspoon grated lemon rind

Grate the cocoanut, add the water and squeeze in a piece of cloth to extract the milk. Add sugar and lemon rind. Freeze.

COCOANUT AND CHERRY ICE CREAM   15 servings

2 egg yolks beaten	1 cup cherries
½ cup sugar	1 cup undiluted evaporated milk
¼ teaspoon salt	
1 quart milk	2 beaten egg whites
1 cup cocoanut milk	

To yolks add sugar, salt and a quart of milk. Cook in a double boiler until mixture coats the spoon. Remove from heat and let cool. Remove seeds and mash cherries. Add cocoanut milk, cherries pulp, evaporated milk and beaten whites to milk. Mix well and freeze.

COFFEE ICE CREAM   15 servings

4 egg yolks   ½ teaspoon salt
4 cups hot milk   ½ cup dripped coffee
1 cup sugar

Beat yolks, add sugar and milk. Cook in double boiler until it gets thick. Let cool, add coffee and mix well. Freeze.

GINGER ICE CREAM   20 servings

4 ounces ginger   8 cups milk
2 cups water   2½ cups sugar

Wash ginger and cut in small pieces. Boil in water for few minutes. Strain and cool. Add sugar to milk and the cold ginger tea. Freeze.

GUAVA ICE   15 servings

2 pounds ripe guavas   3 cups water
2 cups sugar

Wash and peel guavas, cut in halves. Remove pulp, mash and strain. Add water and sugar to the pulp. Freeze.

ICE CREAM   15 servings
Mantecado

4 eggs   1 tablespoon vanilla
1 cup sugar   ½ teaspoon salt
5 cups milk

Beat whole eggs, add sugar and milk. Cook in double boiler, for 4 minutes, stirring constantly until mixture thickens, add salt. Strain, add vanilla and cool. Freeze.

LEMON ICE   15 servings

½ cup lemon juice   4 cups cold milk
2 cups sugar

Mix sugar and lemon juice and let cool in the refrigerator. To the cold milk add the cold lemon juice. Freeze.

[21]

MANGO ICE   10 servings

    3 cups mango pulp   1 cup sugar
    1 cup water   2 tablespoons lemon juice

Mix water and pulp and strain. Add sugar and lemon juice. Freeze.

MERINGUE MILK   12 servings
Leche Merengada

    4 cups milk   5 beaten egg whites
    Peel of 1 lemon   1¼ cups sugar

Boil the milk with lemon peel. Remove peel, add sugar and egg whites gradually. Cook in double boiler for 5 minutes. Strain and cool. Freeze.

ORANGE ICE   15 servings

Substitute the lemon juice of Lemon Ice for 1 cup orange juice. If the orange juice is too sweet, add one or two tablespoons of lemon juice.

PINEAPPLE ICE   15 servings

    2 cups pineapple juice   1 cup sugar
    2 cups water

Make a light syrup with water and sugar. Let cool and add the pineapple juice. Freeze.

SOURSOP ICE CREAM   20 servings

    2 cups soursop pulp   5 cups milk
    1½ cups sugar

Mash pulp with sugar and add milk. If the soursop is very sweet add 2 tablespoons lemon juice. Strain and freeze.

For other fruit recipes please see Chapters IX and X.

CHAPTER III

SOUPS

The word soup suggests something hot, appetizing and stimulating. Soups should have good flavor, the proper consistency and attractive appearance.

It was a tradition to serve soup as the first course at luncheon and dinner, but this good old practice is disappearing. Gone are the days of the elaborate meals with several dishes and its accompaniments. As meals are simpler now, in many homes soup is served only at dinner.

The thin soups or consommes may be served as an appetizer or at the beginning of a full meal. The thick heavy soups such as "sopones" "sancocho" "cocido" and "rancho" are served as the main course to a meal. For lack of an equivalent name in English to sopones we are calling them "stew". The "sopón" can make a wonderful meal served with salad and dessert.

MEAT BROTH   6 servings

1 pound beef brisket	1 onion, diced
½ pound bones	2 chopped cloves garlic
4 cups cold water	1 sprig parsley
1 tablespoon salt	1 tomato cut in pieces
2 carrots cut into small pieces	2 ounces smoked ham, cut in
1 chopped green pepper	pieces

Cut meat into small pieces. Add the meat and bones to the cold water and let stand for not less than half an hour. Add all the other ingredients and place over the heat. As soon as it begins to boil, lower the heat and let simmer for about two hours. Strain and season to taste. Serve hot.

MEAT BROTH II

6 servings

1 pound bones	2 tablespoons salt
1 pound beef brisket	1 tablespoon lard
1 pound chicken cut in pieces	1 chopped onion
¼ pound chopped ham	1 bay leaf
8 cups water	1 sprig parsley

Cut meat into small pieces and brown in the fat. Add the brown meat, bones, chicken and ham to the cold water. Allow to stand half an hour. Add the remaining ingredients and place over the heat. As soon as it boils, lower the heat and let simmer for two hours. Strain, season and serve hot.

VERMICELLI SOUP

6 servings

6 cups broth	2 medium sized pared potatoes
1 ounce vermicelli cut into	cut in quarters
1 inch pieces	

Heat broth to boiling point add vermicelli and potatoes and cook until the potatoes are done, about 20 minutes. See illustration.

CASSAVA SOUP

6 servings

6 cups broth	½ cup ground cassava

Add cassava to the broth and stir well. Set over the heat and stir until it thickens. Strain and serve hot.

PLANTAIN SOUP

6 servings

6 cups broth	½ green plantain

Grate the plantain and add to the broth while stirring. Cook over a low heat until it thickens. Season, strain and serve hot.

GARLIC AND EGG SOUP

6 servings

3 tablespoons olive oil	6 slices toast
6 cloves garlic	6 eggs
6 cups broth[1]	

Fry the garlic and when golden brown remove from the oil and add

---

[1] Hot water seasoned with salt may be used in place of broth.

broth. When·the broth boils add the eggs one at a time and simmer to cook eggs. Place a toast on each soup plate and place an egg on top of each toast, and pour over broth.

CHICKEN SOUP   6 servings

1–2 pounds chicken	1 tablespoon salt
2 ounces chopped smoked ham	½ pound pared, quartered potatoes
1 sliced onion	
2 cloves garlic	2 ounces vermicilli cut into 1″ pieces
8 cups water	

Divide the chicken into pieces at joints. Add to the water, with ham, garlic, onion and salt. Let stand for half an hour. Place over the heat and when it boils reduce the heat and simmer until the chicken is tender. Strain. Add potatoes, vermicelli and chicken pieces. Cook until the potatoes are done.

PIGEON SOUP   6 servings
Sopa de Paloma

3 pigeons,·ready to cook	2 ounces chopped ham
8 cups water	Salt to taste
1 sliced onion	2 pared, quartered potatoes
1 clove garlic	¼ cup rice

Cut the pigeons in halves, add water, onion, garlic and ham. Let stand for half an hour. Place over the heat until it boils, then reduce the heat and simmer until the pigeons are tender. Strain. Add rice, potatoes and pigeons. Season and cook until the rice and potatoes are done.

PLANTAIN BALL SOUP   6 servings

7 cups broth	1 sprig parsley
2 green plantains	1 pound pared, small potatoes
2 ripe plantains	Salt to taste

Peel the green plantains and place in salted water for five minutes. To the hot broth add the green plantains, potatoes and parsley. When the plantains are done, mash and shape into balls. Add to broth. Use salted water to boil the ripe plantains. When done mash and form into balls and add to broth. Season and serve hot.

GALICIAN BROTH[2]
Caldo Gallego

6 servings

1-2 pounds chicken, ready to cook
6 cups water
½ pound fresh navy beans
1 pound lean beaf
½ pound smoked ham
1 sliced onion
3 cloves garlic

1 bunch turnips
¼ pound salt pork
½ pound tomatoes
1 tablespoon salt
1 pound pared, halved potatoes
1 pound cabbage cut into 1" pieces

Divide the chicken into pieces at joints, cut the beef, ham and salt pork into small pieces. To the water add meats, beans, onion, garlic and tomatoes and cook to a broth. Season and add potatoes, turnips and cabbage. When these vegetables are done and before serving add about a tablespoon of olive oil and a teaspoon of vinegar or sour orange juice.

SOFRITO

½ cup

2 ounces salt pork
2 ounces smoked ham
1 chopped green pepper
1 chopped tomato

1 chopped onion
1 ground clove garlic
1 teaspoon salt

Sauté ham and salt pork then add all other ingredients and cook over low heat for about five minutes. Keep in a covered glass container in refrigerator to use as needed.

PIGEON PEA STEW

6 servings

1 pound fresh pigeon peas
6 cups water
1 cup rice
1 cup "sofrito"

½ pound pared, quartered potatoes
1 pound pumpkin cut into 1" cubes
1 tablespoon salt

Cook pigeon peas until tender, add "sofrito", rice and vegetables. Season and cook over a low heat until the rice is tender and serve as soon as it is done.

---

[2] This dish although called broth is really a thick soup.

NOTE: Pigeon peas may be substituted by chick peas, beans or cowpeas.

VEGETABLE STEW
Sancocho

8 servings

1 pound flank
½ pound pork shoulder
8 cups water
2 ounces chopped ham
1 chopped onion
2 chopped tomatoes
1 chopped green pepper
2 chopped sweet peppers
½ pound yautia cut into 1½"
 cubes
½ pound pumpkin cut into
 1½" cubes

½ pound pared, halved potatoes
½ pound yam cut into 1½"
 cubes
1 green plantain cut into ½"
 slices
1 ripe plantain cut into ½"
 slices
2 ears of green corn, cut into 1"
 slices
1 sprig cilantro
1 tablespoon salt

Cut meat into 1" cubes and cover with cold water. Add pork, ham, onion, tomatoes, peppers, seasoning herbs and salt. Cook at simmering temperature until the meat is tender. Season, add vegetables and cook until vegetables are tender.

SOLDIERS' STEW
Rancho

8 servings

1 pound flank
6 cups water
1 chopped onion
1 chopped tomato
1 chopped green pepper
1 pound chick peas (place in water over night)
1 pound cabbage cut into 1"
 pieces

½ pound pared, quartered
 potatoes
1 pound pumpkin cut into
 1" cubes
1 tablespoon salt
½ cup noodles cut into 1"
 pieces

Cut the meat into 1" cubes and cover with cold water, add chick peas, onion, pepper and tomato. Cook at simmering temperature until the meat and chick peas are tender. Add vegetables and noodles. Season and cook until the vegetables are done.

[27]

SPANISH STEW
Cocido
8 servings

1 pound flank cut into 1½"
cubes
6 cups water
1 chopped onion
2 chopped tomatoes
2 chopped green peppers
1 chopped clove garlic
¼ pound chopped smoked ham
½ pound cabbage cut into 1"
pieces

3 pared carrots cut into 1"
slices
1 pound chick peas (place in
water overnight)
1 tablespoon salt
2 Spanish sausages cut into 1"
pieces
1 pound pared, halved potatoes
½ pound string beans cut into
1" pieces

Cover meat with cold water, add ham, chick peas, onion, green peppers, garlic and tomato. Simmer until meat and chick peas are tender. Add sausages and vegetables. Season and cook until vegetables are tender. See illustration.

GAZPACHO
6 servings

1 clove garlic
½ teaspoon pepper corns
½ teaspoon salt
3 tablespoons olive oil
4 cups cold water
2 tablespoons vinegar

4 chopped tomatoes
2 chopped onions
2 chopped cucumbers
2 chopped green peppers
½ cup cubed bread

Grind pepper corns, garlic and salt in a mortar. Add water, oil and vinegar. Strain and add tomatoes, onions, cucumbers and green peppers. Keep in refrigerator and add bread before serving.

CHAPTER IV

MEAT AND POULTRY

Meat

As Puerto Rico does not produce enough meat to supply the demand, a great deal of meat as well as other foodstuffs are imported. In the grocery stores you will find American cuts of meat, imported poultry and fish, besides those produced in the Island.

The best Puerto Rican cuts are the tenderloin and loin (filete and lomillo). The hind leg contains the following cuts: the "babilla",[1] the "lechón or gansillo",[2] and "masa larga".

The following table includes the names of the Puerto Rican cuts and their English equivalents, as well as their uses.

COMPARISON OF PUERTO RICAN AND AMERICAN CUTS OF MEAT

English Name	Spanish Name	Description	Use
Shank	Garrón		Soup
Round	Babilla	Upper part of round	Pot roast, stew, hash, steak
Eye of the round	Lechón o gansillo	Lower side of round	Larded meat
Loin	Lomillo	Upper part of short loin	Beefsteak, meat loaf
Tenderloin	Filete		Roast beef, filet mignon
Chuck	Espalda		Ground, pot roast, stew
Rump	Cadera	Same as in U. S.	Ground, stew, beefsteak
Flank	Faldilla	Same as in U. S.	Hash, soup, stew
Brisket	Pecho	Same as in U. S.	Soup, stew

Beef fresh, canned or dried is consumed more than any other kind of meat. Pork is very popular because ground pork is used for several dishes such as: stuffed vegetables, turnovers, vegetable pies, and boiled plantain "pasteles". Rump, round or flank may be used for

---

[1] Top of round.

[2] Is known in Puerto Rico by these two names; in the U. S. as "the eye of the round". Is the best cut for "Larded Meat"

grinding. Baked fresh ham is a choice dish; fried pork chops with "tostones" is a very common food combination. The pork rind is used for "chicharrones" (cracklings).

Smoked ham is cut up in pieces and added to the "sofrito" which is a basic ingredient or seasoning for many dishes.

A meat considered a delicacy is "carne de cabrito" (meat from the young kid of the goat), but it is not available in the market as it is not produced on a commercial scale. It may be especially ordered from some meat dealer. Rabbit meat has a mild flavor and is fine grained; it is becoming more available and is a means of adding variety to the menus. There are some rabbit farms near Bayamón where this meat can be ordered. Because of its flavor and tenderness, rabbit can be prepared the same as chicken. Seasoned and cooked properly, there is not much difference from chicken and turkey flavor.

The variety meats, brains, heart, kidney, liver, tongue and tripe, are marketed here; some of these meats are imported and may be bought frozen.

The native sausages, "butifarras" and "longaniza", are made from lean pork meat; "morcilla" is a blood sausage made from the blood of the pork. Morcilla as well as gandinga is a rich source of iron salts and vitamins.

Fresh or pickled pigs feet are found at the stores and the market, also veal, both chops and leg of veal.

BOILED

OLD CLOTHES   8 servings
Ropa Vieja

Left-over soup meat, about 2 pounds	2 tablespoons fat
	1 tablespoon capers
2 chopped tomatoes	2 chopped cloves garlic
2 chopped peppers	2 teaspoons salt
2 sliced onions	

Remove sinews from meat and season it with salt and garlic. Brown the onions, tomatoes and peppers slightly and add the meat and capers. Cook over a low heat. It is usually served with French fried potatoes.

[30]

DRIED BEEF WITH TOMATOES   6 servings

1½ pounds dried beef	2 sliced onions
3 tablespoons fat	1 clove chopped garlic
1 pound chopped tomatoes	2 sliced peppers
Salt to taste	

Soak the dried beef in water two or three hours. Cut it into pieces and boil until tender. Drain and mince. Sauté the tomatoes, onions and peppers and add the chopped garlic. Add the meat. Stir well together and cover. Cook over low heat for 15 minutes.

NOTE: Serve with fried potatoes or with boiled vegetables.

DRIED BEEF WITH EGGS   6 servings

1½ pounds dried beef	5 beaten eggs
3 tablespoons fat	½ teaspoon salt
2 sliced onions	

Cut the dried beef into pieces and soak for two hours. Boil until tender. Cut up fine. Sauté the onion without letting it brown. Add the meat and mix together well. Cook over a low heat for ten minutes. Add the beaten eggs and stir slowly until eggs are cooked. Serve hot.

BOILED HAM IN WINE   15–20 servings

1–8 to 10 pounds partially cooked ham	4 sticks cinnamon
	1 teaspoon whole cloves
1½ pounds brown sugar	1 quart red Spanish wine

Mix sugar, cinnamon, cloves and wine; add to ham with fat side up. Cook in a shallow open pan, over low heat. Turn occasionally until the ham is tender. Cooking time about 3 hours. Serve cold sliced with wine sauce.

STEW

ACHOTE COLORING

½ cup fat	¼ cup annato seeds

Wash the annato seeds. Heat lard and add seeds. Simmer for ten minutes. Strain and when cool place in a covered glass bottle and keep in refrigerator. Add to stews, soup and other dishes for coloring.

BEEF STEW
6 servings

1½ pounds shoulder beef
1 tablespoon salt
2 sliced tomatoes
2 sliced peppers
2 sliced onions

3 cloves chopped garlic
4 tablespoons achote coloring
1 tablespoon vinegar
1½ pounds potatoes

Clean the meat and cut into 1½ inches cubes. Season with garlic, salt and vinegar. Put it into a kettle and add the other ingredients. Stir well and add the cup of water and the potatoes. Cook over a low heat until meat is tender.

POT ROAST
10 servings

2½ pounds rump
1 clove chopped garlic
1½ tablespoons salt
2 tablespoons chopped onion

1 tablespoon vinegar
4 tablespoons fat
2 cups water
1½ pounds pared small potatoes

Clean the meat. Make small incisions with a sharp pointed knife. Mix together the garlic, salt, onion, and the vinegar and rub the meat on all sides. Do not cut up meat. Brown meat in hot fat. Add the water, cover and cook over a low heat until tender. Add the potatoes to the meat before the liquid has evaporated. Leave over low heat until the meat is tender and the potatoes are done.

LARDED MEAT
Carne Mechada
8–10 servings

1–2–3 pounds eye of the
   round (lechón)
¼ pound ham
¼ pound salt pork
1 chopped onion
1 tablespoon minced capers
1 cup hot water

¼ cup tomato sauce
¼ cup pitted olives
1 chopped clove garlic
1 tablespoon salt
1 tablespoon vinegar
¼ cup fat
6 pared halved potatoes

Rub all sides of the meat with salt, and garlic and add vinegar. Cut ham and salt pork into 1″ strips. Mix with onion, capers and olives. With a fine sharp knife make an incision through the center of the meat, and lard it with ham, salt pork and vegetables. Fry meat and brown on both sides. Add water, tomato sauce and season to taste. Cover kettle and cook slowly at a low heat. When meat is tender add potatoes and remove from heat when potatoes are done and the gravy thick. Slice and serve with potatoes. See illustration.

KETTLE COOKED FRESH HAM   12–14 servings

5 or 6 pounds fresh ham	2 cloves chopped garlic
2 tablespoons salt	2 tablespoons vinegar
¼ teaspoon pepper	½ cup fat
1 teaspoon powdered marjoram (orégano)	2 cups water

Make incisions in the meat with a fine, sharp knife. Mix the salt, pepper, marjoram and garlic and stuff these condiments into the incisions, and rub meat on all sides. Pour the vinegar over the meat and allow to stand 3 or 4 hours, or, if possible, all night. Heat the lard and brown the meat on all sides. Cover with water, reduce heat, and turn over from time to time. Cooking time is about 2 to 3 hours.

BAKED FRESH HAM   See illustration
Pernil al Horno

Follow directions for seasoning Kettle Cooked Fresh Ham, but omit vinegar. Place in a covered roasting pan and bake at 350° F for 2 hours. Remove lid and brown 15 minutes before ham is done.

RABBIT STEW   6 servings

1–3 pound rabbit	1 bay leaf
2 tablespoons salt	1 cup olive oil
½ teaspoon marjoram	¼ cup sherry
2 cloves garlic	1 pound pared small potatoes
½ cup olives	¼ pound chopped ham
½ pound small whole onions	2 chopped tomatoes

Wash the rabbit in water with either lemon or sour orange juice. Cut up and rub with salt. Put it into a kettle with the marjoram, garlic, onion, ham, olives, bay leaf, oil and tomatoes. Stir well together and put over a low heat for 20 minutes. Add the wine and continue cooking for one hour. The potatoes should be added 15 minutes before cooking time is over.

RABBIT WITH SHERRY   6 servings

1–3 pound rabbit dressed and cut up	1 tablespoon flour
3 tablespoons salt	¼ cup Sherry
4 tablespoons fat	1 cup water
3 ounces chopped ham	1 bay leaf
1 ounce chopped salt pork	6 peppercorns
1 chopped onion	2 cloves
1 whole clove garlic	Salt to taste
1 tablespoon minced parsley	½ cup sherry

Rub the rabbit with salt and brown in fat. Add the ham, salt pork, onion, parsley and the garlic. Sauté together over a low heat, add the flour and stir well, then add the ¼ cup sherry and the cup of water. Cook a while. Remove from heat and strain the sauce. Put rabbit back into kettle and add the sauce. Add the bay leaf, pepper, cloves and salt to taste and cook over low heat until meat is tender. Add the remaining ½ cup of wine a few minutes before serving.

YOUNG KID STEW   8 servings

4 pounds kid meat	¼ pound chopped ham
1 sour orange	½ cup olives
3 tablespoons salt	1 tablespoon capers
2 chopped garlic	1 bay leaf
½ teaspoon pepper or marjoram	1 cup olive oil
2 tablespoons vinegar	1 cup chopped tomatoes
½ pound small onions	4 pimentos
¼ pound chopped salt pork	1 cup Spanish red wine

Clean the meat and rinse in water with sour orange juice. Cut meat up and season it with the salt, garlic, pepper and vinegar. Add all the other ingredients except the wine and stir well together. Cook covered, over low heat until the meat is tender. Add the wine just before removing from heat.

YOUNG KID HUNTERS' STYLE   6–8 servings

4 pounds young kid meat
1 sour orange
3 tablespoons salt
2 chopped cloves garlic
½ cup fat
½ teaspoon pepper

1 chopped onion
¼ pound chopped salt pork
1 bay leaf
1 cup white wine
1 tablespoon minced parsley

Clean the meat and wash with the juice of the sour orange. Cut into pieces and season several hours before cooking. Heat the fat and brown the meat, add the onion, salt pork, bay leaf, and cook over moderate heat for ten minutes, stirring it occasionally. Add the wine and cook until the meat is tender. Add the parsley before serving.

GANDINGA   8 servings

2 pounds gandinga
2 chopped onions
2 chopped tomatoes
2 chopped peppers
1 chopped sweet pepper
1 sprig minced cilantrillo
1 chopped clove garlic
1 cup water

¼ teaspoon powdered orégano
1½ teaspoons salt
1 tablespoon vinegar
1 tablespoon achote coloring
1 tablespoon capers
½ cup olives
1 pound pared quartered potatoes

Cut gandinga into 1 inch cubes, add the onion, tomatoes, peppers, cilantrillo, garlic, orégano, salt, water and vinegar. Stir together well. Add the lard, capers and olives. Cook over a low heat for 45 minutes. Add potatoes and serve when the potatoes are done.

TRIPE STEW   6 servings
Mondongo

1½ pounds tripe
1 sour orange juice
1 chopped pepper
1 chopped onion
2 chopped tomatoes
2 tablespoons fat
¼ pound chopped ham
1 chopped sweet pepper
4 cups water

2½ teaspoons salt
2 leaves cilantro
1 sprig parsley
½ teaspoon achote coloring
½ pound pumpkin, cut into 1″ cubes
¾ pound pared halved potatoes
1 cup cooked garbanzos

Wash tripe with the sour orange juice, cover with water, boil a few

[35]

minutes and drain. Cut the tripe into small pieces. Prepare a "sofrito" with the pepper, onion, tomatoes, ham, sweet pepper and seasoning herbs. Add the "sofrito", the water, the garbanzos and the salt. Cook over low heat until tripe is tender. Add the potatoes and the pumpkin. Remove from heat when they are done.

PIGS' FEET STEW   6 servings

2 pounds salted pigs' feet[4]
½ pound chick peas[5]
6 cups water
2 teaspoons salt
1 chopped pepper
½ pound pumpkin cut into 1" cubes

1 chopped onions
2 ounces chopped ham
1 sliced Spanish sausage
2 leaves cilantro
1 tablespoon achote coloring
½ pound pared halved potatoes
2 chopped tomatoes

Cut up the pigs' feet and soak them for several hours. Boil the feet and the chick peas until they are almost tender. Prepare a "sofrito" with the lard, pepper, onion, tomatoes and ham. Add the "sofrito", salt, chorizo and cilantro to the pigs' feet. Cook over moderate heat. Add the potatoes and the pumpkin, season to taste and remove from heat when they are done.

KIDNEY STEW   6 servings

1½ pounds kidneys
½ cup tomato sauce
2 minced onions
½ tablespoon salt

1 chopped clove garlic
1 tablespoon vinegar
4 tablespoons olive oil

Remove all fat from the kidneys. Cut them in two and put into a hot kettle over a low heat and whenever the kidneys secrete any liquid, remove it with absorbent paper. Remove from heat, wash and cut kidneys into small pieces. Mix the tomato sauce, onion, salt, garlic, vinegar and the olive oil together with the kidneys. Cook over low heat for 20 minutes and serve at once.

---

[4] If fresh pigs' feet are used, season the preceding day.

[5] In some towns of the Island, they do not use Spanish sausage, chick peas or pumpkin in this recipe.

KIDNEY STEW WITH SHERRY   6 servings

1½ pounds kidneys   ½ tablespoon salt
1 chopped onion   ⅛ teaspoon pepper
4 tablespoons butter or olive   2 tablespoons flour
    oil   ½ cup sherry

Clean the kidneys, following instructions in preceding recipe. Sauté
the onion in the butter or the olive oil and add the kidneys, salt and
pepper. Cook over low heat for 20 minutes. Add the wine. Serve as
soon as done.

FRIED

FILET MIGNON   4–6 servings

2 pounds tenderloin   ¼ teaspoon pepper
1 tablespoon salt   6 strips bacon

Clean the tenderloin and cut in slices about 1½ inches thick. Rub
with salt and pepper. Arrange a strip of bacon around each slice, and
broil for 10 minutes. Serve with mushroom sauce, onions or peas.

ROAST BEEF   6 servings

2 pounds tenderloin   ½ grated onion
3 cloves garlic   1 tablespoon vinegar
1 tablespoon salt   2 tablespoons olive oil

Mash garlic, salt and add onion. Clean the tenderloin and season it
whole. Heat the oil. Put in the meat and brown it. Cover and lower
the heat. Cook for 15 or 20 minutes.

TENDERLOIN STUFFED WITH   6 servings
VEGETABLES

2½ pounds tenderloin   4 cooked carrots chopped
1½ tablespoons salt   3 chopped pimentos
3 cloves garlic   4 tablespoons flour
½ chopped onion   ¼ cup fat
2 tablespoons olive oil   1 tablespoon vinegar
¼ pound cooked string beans

Clean tenderloin and leave it whole. Slash down its length, then make two more slashes, one on each side of first so that the loin lies flat in rectangular shape. Mash the garlic and mix it with the salt, onion, oil and vinegar. Rub the loin on both sides. Stuff in the vegetables and tie it together from end to end. Sprinkle it with flour and brown it in the lard. Cover and cook over low heat until loin is done.

BEEFSTEAK   6 servings

1½ pounds loin	¼ teaspoon pepper
2 cloves garlic	2 sliced onions
1 tablespoon salt	Fat for frying
1 tablespoon vinegar	

Cut the meat into six pieces, crosswise. Pound it gently. Mash the garlic, mix the salt and pepper and add the vinegar. Season the meat, cover with the sliced onion. Let stand several hours. Fry the steaks in hot fat. Brown the onions and serve at once.

NOTE: If desired, the garlic and vinegar may be omitted from the seasoning.

BREADED BEEFSTEAK   6 servings

1½ pounds loin	3 beaten eggs
2 mashed cloves garlic	½ teaspoon salt
1 tablespoon salt	1 cup cracker crumbs
¼ teaspoon pepper	Fat for frying

Cut the loin into steaks about ½ inch thick and pound lightly. Mix garlic, salt and pepper. Rub each steak with seasoning on both sides. Dip each steak first in egg and then in cracker crumbs, place over each steak a piece of parafin paper and press lightly, so crumbs will stick. Fry in hot lard until brown, drain on absorbent paper.

MEAT BALLS   6 servings

1 pound ground beef	1 teaspoon salt
¼ pound chopped ham	1 beaten egg
1 chopped onion	½ cup flour
1 slice of bread	¼ cup fat
¼ teaspoon nutmeg	1 cup tomato sauce

Moisten the bread with milk or broth and mix it with the chopped ingredients. Add the egg, nutmeg and salt, and mix well. Shape the meat into balls and roll them in flour. Brown in hot lard and add the sauce. Cook balls over low heat for 15 minutes.

CRACKLINGS
Chicharrones

Cut pork skin up into small pieces and leave them in cold water for an hour or two. Drain the pig skin and cook in a kettle, over medium heat. When the skin has rendered considerable fat, remove it. Fry until the skins begin to brown then sprinkle with salted water so they will puff up. When light brown drain on absorbent paper.

FRIED RABBIT   6 servings

3—2 to 2½ pounds rabbit	1 teaspoon pepper
2 sour oranges	2 tablespoons salt
3 cloves garlic	Fat for frying

Wash the rabbit with sour orange or lemon juice. Disjoint the rabbit. Pound or grind the garlic and mix with the salt and pepper. Rub the pieces hours before frying. Fry in hot lard until brown. Reduce the heat, cover and cook slowly for 45 minutes.

BREADED BRAINS   6 servings

2 brains	Salt and pepper to taste
2 beaten eggs	Fat for frying
2 tablespoons flour	

Boil the brains in salted water. Clean and slice. Sprinkle with salt and pepper. Dip each slice in egg, then in flour and fry in hot fat.

LINK SAUSAGE   24–30 sausages

3 pounds lean pork meat	½ teaspoon nutmeg
1 teaspoon pepper	2 yards dry pork intestines

Grind the pork, add the salt, pepper and nutmeg to the ground meat and mix well. Stuff the intestines and tie every two inches. Prick each sausage with a pin. Boil the sausages for 3 minutes. Drain and hang it up to dry.

PLAIN SAUSAGES

3 pounds pork meat	1 teaspoon powdered marjoram
3 tablespoons salt	(orégano)
½ teaspoon pepper	½ cup achote coloring
4 mashed cloves garlic	2 yards dry pork intestines

Grind the meat. Add the salt, pepper, garlic, marjoram and the achote coloring to the meat. Mix well together and stuff the intestine using a wide, long funnel. Prick the sausage to permit some fat to drain out and hang it up to dry.

NOTE: When the pork intestine has been cleaned; fill it with air and hang it up to dry, before stuffing; so it will not stick.

AJILIMÓJILI SAUCE

3 chili peppers	4 cloves garlic
3 sweet peppers	½ cup oil
1 teaspoon salt	½ cup lemon juice
4 peppercorns	

Grind up together the chili peppers and the garlic with the salt and pepper. Add the oil and the lemon juice, stir well and strain.

POULTRY

Chicken (pollos) are plentiful because there are several poultry farms near large urban centers. Turkeys are raised also but are most abundant about November to January for Thanksgiving and Christmas holidays. Chicken and turkey are also imported.

Hens (gallinas) are preferred for soups and some dishes which require large, mature animals. Its flavor develops during long cooking at a low temperature.

Guinea hen (guinea) are found occasionally at the market. The flesh of the guinea hen is a little drier than chicken but tenderer; it is usually cooked in fricassee and served with rice.

Squabs (palomas) have a delicate flavor and are cooked the same as chicken; one squab, about a pound, should be allowed per person.

FRIED CHICKEN   6 servings
Pollo Frito

3—1½ to 2 pounds ready to   3 tablespoons salt
cook chicken, cut up   ½ teaspoon pepper
3 cloves garlic   Fat for frying

Split the chickens down the back. Pound or grind the garlic with the salt and pepper and rub the chicken in and outside and set in a cool place for an hour or more. Brown in hot fat. Lower the heat, cover and cook 30 minutes, turn once or twice before removing from heat.

CHICKEN WITH MILK   6 servings

1–2½ pounds ready to cook   2 cups hot water
  chicken   1 tablespoon salt
4 ounces fat   2 cups milk
½ pound sliced onions   ¼ pound butter

Do not cut up or split the chicken. Sauté it until browned. Add the onions and the water. Season to taste. Cover and cook over low heat. Half an hour before removing from heat, add the milk and the butter. Serve when the sauce is thick.

CHICKEN WITH ONIONS   6 servings

1–3 pounds ready to cook   1 cup olive oil
  chicken, cut up[6]   Salt to taste
1 pound sliced onions

Rub the chicken with salt. Put the olive oil in the kettle, place the sliced onion and chicken on top of the onions. Cover and cook over low heat for one hour. Turn chicken over twice.

---

[6] Chicken may be either cut up or whole.

[41]

PICKLED CHICKEN
Pollo en Escabeche

6–8 servings

1–3 pounds ready to cook
   chicken, cut up
1 tablespoon salt
½ teaspoon pepper
1 bay leaf

1 cup olive oil
4 tablespoons butter
½ pound sliced onions
½ cup vinegar

Rub the chicken with the salt and pepper. Brown in the olive oil. Arrange the slices of onion over the chicken and add the butter, bay leaf and vinegar. Cover and cook over low heat until the chicken is tender.

PICKLED PIGEONS

Follow directions for Pickled Chicken.

CHICKEN FRICASSEE
Fricasé de Pollo

6–8 servings

1–3 pounds ready to cook
   chicken, cut up
1 tablespoon salt
½ teaspoon marjoram (oré-
   gano)
2 cloves minced garlic
¼ teaspoon pepper
2 tablespoons vinegar
¼ pound chopped ham

1 bay leaf
½ cup olive oil
½ cup tomato sauce
1 pound pared quartered potatoes
3 ounces sliced onions
½ cup olives
1 tablespoon capers
2 pimentos

Mix salt, marjoram, garlic, pepper and vinegar and rub chicken three hours before cooking. Place in kettle with other ingredients except olives, capers and potatoes. Stir, cover and cook over low heat. Stir two or three times. When chicken is almost tender add olives, capers and potatoes. Remove from heat when potatoes are tender.

NOTE: Guinea hens may be used also, instead of chicken.

[42]

HEN IN ALMOND SAUCE
Gallina en Pepitoria

6–8 servings

1–4 pounds ready to cook hen cut up	2 sprigs minced parsley
Salt to taste	5 peppercorns
1 cup olive oil or lard	5 cloves
1 chopped tomato	½ teaspoon cinnamon
1 chopped onion	½ pound almonds
2 cups warm water	½ teaspoon lemon juice
1 minced clove garlic	2 egg yolks

Rub each chicken piece with salt and sauté in olive oil. Add the tomato, onion and water and cook over low heat. When the hen is almost done, add the condiments and allow to boil again. Remove and set aside the pieces of chicken, and strain the sauce. Grind the almonds, extract the milk and add to the sauce. Place chicken in kettle and pour over the sauce and boil for several minutes. Add the beaten yolks and lemon juice to the sauce a few minutes before servings.

SOUR-SWEET HEN
Gallina a lo Agridulce

6–8 servings

1–3 pounds ready to cook hen	3 tablespoons fat
1 tablespoon salt	4 ounces chopped ham
½ teaspoon pepper	2 Spanish sausages
2 chopped cloves garlic	4 cups water
1 tablespoon vinegar	1 cup brown sugar
2 tablespoons olive oil	½ cup vinegar

Rub hen inside and out with salt, pepper, garlic, vinegar and olive oil and leave over night. Put the fat into a kettle and add the hen, ham and sausages. Mix the water, sugar and vinegar together and pour over the hen. Cover and cook over low heat turning occasionally until the hen is tender and the gravy thick.

STUFFED BAKED CHICKEN   6 servings

1–4 pounds ready to cook chicken

3 teaspoons salt

2 cloves chopped garlic

½ teaspoon powdered marjoram

1 chopped onion

1½ pounds pork meat

¼ pound ham

3 tablespoons butter

2 tablespoons tomato sauce

1 tablespoon raisins

½ cup olives

Mix the salt, garlic, marjoram and onion. Rub the chicken inside and out several hours before stuffing. Grind the pork meat and ham and add the rest of the ingredients. Season to taste and stuff the chicken. Sew up opening and rub the skin with butter or achote coloring. Place chicken in uncovered baking pan into the oven at 400° F and when it has browned lower temperature to 325° F, cover and bake for 2 hours. Baste with drippings or melted butter from time to time.

STUFFED TURKEY   12 to 16 servings

1–8 pounds ready to cook turkey

Seasoning

4 tablespoons salt

2 minced cloves garlic

½ teaspoon pepper

3 tablespoons olive oil

2 tablespoons vinegar

Stuffing:

3 pounds pork meat

1½ pounds ham

1 pound bread, moistened in broth

1½ teaspoons ground bay leaves

½ cup sherry

1 teaspoon pepper

½ cup melted butter

¾ cup whole almonds

Mix salt, garlic and pepper and rub turkey inside and out. Keep in refrigerator until next day. Grind the meat, ham, giblet, heart and liver. Add the other ingredients, season to taste and mix well. Stuff neck and body cavity loosely as during roasting stuffing absorbs juices and expands. Sew it up and truss. Place turkey with breast side up, on wire rack in roasting pan. Bake at 400° F for 20 minutes; reduce heat to 350° and cover pan. Turn turkey over once or twice and baste with drippings or melted butter. Cooking time about 2 hours.

[44]

TURKEY WITH TRUFFLES
Pavo Trufado

10–12 servings

1–8 pounds ready to cook turkey	1½ pounds boiled ham
1 cup dry wine	1 teaspoon nutmeg
1 can truffles	1 teaspoon pepper
2 onions	½ cup sherry
1 ground bay leaf	1 cup cracker crumbs
1 tablespoon salt	5 beaten eggs

Open the turkey lengthwise down the back. Cut off wings and legs. Remove the skin with a very sharp knife without breaking the skin and put away in the refrigerator. Remove flesh from all bones and season with salt and add wine, and put into refrigerator until following day. Grind meat and boiled ham and add the other ingredients. Mix well together and season. Sew up wing and leg openings in skin and stuff the turkey. Sew up skin of back opening. Wrap in a cheese cloth or a napkin and tie ends as for a sausage. Boil for one hour in broth.[7] Let cool and place in the refrigerator over night. Serve cold sliced.

TURKEY SAUSAGE
Embutido de Pavo

10 or 12 servings

1–8 or 10 pounds ready to cook turkey, cut up	1 can truffles (4 ozs.)
½ pound boiled ham	1 can mushrooms (4 ozs.)
8 eggs	4 beaten eggs
½ tablespoon pepper	½ teaspoon salt
2 teaspoons salt	Cracker crumbs
1 teaspoon nutmeg	Broth

Remove the skin and meat from the bones. Grind the turkey meat and ham with the finest cutter. Season the meat and add the eggs whole one by one and beat to mix them well. Slice the truffles and mushrooms and stir them in so that the truffles and mushrooms are well distributed throughout mixture. Form a roll about 2 or 3 inches wide and 6 or 8 inches long. Roll in beaten egg and cracker crumbs.

---

[7] Prepare the broth with turkey bones and left over meat.

Roll up in a piece of cheese cloth or napkin and tie ends. Boil in broth for one hour. Place in the refrigerator and serve cold.

CHICKEN PIE   6 servings
Pastelón de Pollo

Dough
4 cups flour   3 teaspoons baking powder
1½ teaspoons salt   Ice cold water
1 cup lard

Sift the flour, measure, and mix with the salt and baking powder. Cut the lard into the flour with two knives or with the tips of the fingers. If this is done with the fingers, keep always some flour between fingers and lard so that the heat from fingers will not melt the lard. When the lard and flour mixture has become grainy add the cold water in the center, a little at a time and turning the flour toward the center with a fork. Use as much water as needed so that the dough will be firm and smooth but not wet. Chill dough in refrigerator until ready to use. Divide dough into two parts. Roll one part from the center to the sides, giving dough a circular shape. Roll it about ¼ inch thick, and one inch wider than the pie-tin. Place in pie tin and trim edges. Prick bottom with fork so dough will not puff up. Keep in refrigerator until ready to bake.

Filling
1-2 pounds ready to cook   ½ cup olive oil
   chicken, cut up   1 cup tomato sauce
2 teaspoons salt   3 ounces sliced onions
½ teaspoon marjoram (oré-   1 bay leaf
   gano)   ½ cup olives
2 cloves minced garlic   1 tablespoon capers
¼ teaspoon pepper   ½ pound potatoes, cut up
1 tablespoon vinegar
4 tablespoons olive oil

Season the chicken with salt, marjoram, ground garlic, pepper, vinegar and four tablespoons of olive oil. Put ½ cup olive oil and the rest of the ingredients into a kettle with the chicken and cook covered over low heat until the chicken is tender. Add the potatoes a little while

[46]

before removing from heat. Remove bones from chicken and pour into the unbaked shell. Roll out the rest of the dough to cover the pie. Moisten the edge of the dough lining bottom, put on top crust and press edges together with the tines of the fork. Bake in an oven heated to 400° F for 25 or 30 minutes.

For other chicken and meat recipes please see Chapters VI, VII, and VIII.

CHAPTER V

FISH, EGGS AND CHEESE

Fish is abundant in Puerto Rico especially on the southern and eastern coasts; but as fishing is on a small scale, much salted and dried, and some canned and frozen fish is imported.

Fresh fish is abundant in the towns along the coast; the inland towns do not get fish so often. Salted codfish is consumed in large quantities; it is very popular, there are many recipes for preparing it in different ways.

If fish is not carefully handled and refrigerated it decomposes quickly. Fresh fish may be identified by its clear eyes, bright red gills, firm flesh, bright and moist scales and the characteristic odor of fresh fish. Certain kinds of fish that have very sharp teeth, scrape the algaes and shells from the hull of the boats which are made of copper plates, thus scraping bits of copper. If these fish are eaten they may cause serious stomach disturbances. To detect any trace of copper in the fish, insert a silver or silver plated fork into the head, if the fork turns dark, the fish is not suitable for consumption. This may happen in towns where large ships come into port, but this does not often affect the fish because the best fishing grounds are quite far out.

Following is a list of the most common fishes found the year round, grouped by family and in the order of importance.

Groupers (Mero)
Red grouper   mero
Nassau grouper   cherna
Red hind grouper   cabrilla
Snappers (Manchego)
Lane snapper   manchego[1]
Mutton fish   pargo criollo
Red snapper   pargo colorado
Gray snapper   pargo prieto

---

[1] Next to schoolmaster, is the most abundant

Schoolmaster	pargo amarillo[2]
Yellow-tail	Colirubia
Mackerels (Carite)	
Spanish mackerel	carita, carite[3]
King fish	sierra[4]
The goat fishes (Salmonete)	
Red goat fish	salmonete[5]
Yellow goat fish	salmonete amarillo
The grunts	
Yellow grunt	boquicolorado[6]
Common grunt	cachicata[7]
The porgies (Pluma)	
Saucer-eye porgy	pluma[8]
Sheepshead	chopa amarilla[9]
The robalos (Robalos)	
Snook	robalo[10]
The triple-tails (Sama)	
triple-tail	sama[11]
Barracuda (Picua)	
barracuda	picuda, picua
Mullet (Liza)	
mullet	liza, lisa[12]
The wrasse-fishes (Capitán)	
Hog fish	machete
The cutlass-fishes (Machete)	
Cutlas-fish	machete
The pompanos (Pompano)	
Hard Tail	cojinuda, cojinua[13]
Horse-eye jack	jurel[14]

[2] One of the most abundant of the snappers
[3] Very best food fishes
[4] Flesh is firm, excellent flavor
[5] Extensively used as food and highly esteemed
[6] Important food fish
[7] Abundant and valuable food
[8] Excellent food fish
[9] Excellent pan fish
[10] A common food-fish in Puerto Rico
[11] A very good fish
[12] Important food fish held in high esteem. The most abundant mullet
[13] Valued for foods
[14] Commonest species, very abundant

Corcobado	corcobado[15]
Moon-fish	jorobado
Round pompano	palometa[16]

BOILED

FISH AU GRATIN   6 servings

2 pounds pargo cut into 1" cubes	Chopped parsley
1 chopped onion	Salt and pepper to taste
2½ cups water	¼ pound grated Parmesan cheese
1 tablespoon salt	1 pound sliced tomatoes
1 cup fish broth	3 beaten eggs
1 tablespoon flour	Salt to taste

Add salt and chopped onion to the water and place over the heat.
Add fish and cook for 20 minutes. Remove the fish and strain the
liquid. Prepare a sauce with the liquid, flour, chopped parsley, salt
and pepper. Grease a shallow baking dish, cover bottom with a layer
of fish, another of tomato and sauce and sprinkle with cheese. Repeat
until dish is full. Pour the eggs over the surface and sprinkle with
cheese. Bake at 350° F for 30 minutes.

VINAIGRETTE SAUCE

1 tablespoon salt	1 tablespoon olive oil
¼ teaspoon paprika	1 chopped pickled cucumber
2 peppercorns	½ chopped pepper
3 tablespoons vinegar	1 sprig minced parsley

Mix all ingredientes in the order listed.

FISH A LA VINAIGRETTE

1 whole 2-pounds chillo	2 tablespoons lemon juice
1 cup diced potatoes	2 pimentos
4 chopped hard-cooked eggs	French dressing
1 cup peas	Lettuce leaves
1 sliced onion	3 cloves chopped garlic
2 tablespoons salt	½ teaspoon pepper
½ cup vinaigrette sauce	

Season the fish with the salt, pepper and lemon juice, and wrap it

---

[15] Very abundant
[16] Held in high esteem

in a plantain leaf or in cheese cloth. Boil the fish in salted water with onion and cloves of garlic. When tender, drain and place on a serving platter and pour over the French dressing. Mix the potatoes, peas and chopped eggs together and add the vinaigrette sauce. Arrange lettuce leaves on sides of platter and garnish with the mixture of eggs, potatoes and peppers. Serve cold.

RED GROUPER WITH SAUCE   6 servings

1½ pounds red grouper	2 tablespoons butter
1 teaspoon salt	Salt and pepper to taste
2 pounds chopped tomatoes	1 chopped green pepper
1 cup water	1 chopped onion
1 tablespoon flour	3 cups mashed yautía
½ cup fish broth	Chopped parsley

Boil the fish in a small quantity of water, remove bones and mince fish. Set aside the broth. Cook tomatoes in water over low heat until they are tender. Mash tomatoes and strain through a coarse mesh strainer. Melt the butter, add the flour, the tomato sauce and the fish broth and cook in a double boiler for several minutes. Add the fish, pepper and onion to the sauce. Cook until mixture thickens slightly. Season to taste. Form a ring around a serving platter with the mashed yautía, and put the fish inside the ring. Garnish with chopped parsley.

FISH PASTELES   6 pasteles

1 pound yellow yautía	1 chopped onion
6 green bananas[17]	1 chopped pepper
Salt to taste	2 chopped sweet peppers
¼ cup achote coloring	1 chopped hot pepper
½ cup evaporated milk (un-diluted)	Parsley and cilantro, minced
	¼ cup olive oil
1½ pounds mullet[18]	½ cup olives
1 chopped tomato	1 tablespoon capers

Grate the yautía and bananas; add the salt, achote coloring and the milk. Mix until smooth and soft. Boil the fish in a small quantity of water, drain and remove bones. Sauté onion, tomato and peppers,

---

[17] Green plantains may be substituted for the green bananas.
[18] Chillo or robalo or baby sharks may be used.

[51]

add the fish cut into small pieces, the parsley and the cilantro, the olives, capers and the hot peppers. Cook several minutes. Add a little fish broth to avoid dryness. Make the pasteles following directions for Pasteles de Plátano.

FRIED

FRIED FISH   6 servings

3 pounds mullet
Olive oil[19]
Lemon juice

Flour
Salt and pepper to taste
Fat for frying

Slice the fish and season with salt, pepper and lemon juice. Set aside in a cool place for one hour. Flour the slices and fry in sufficient olive oil to brown them uniformly until done. Serve hot.

PICKLED FISH   6 servings
Pescado en Escabeche

6 slices Spanish mackerel
   (carite)
Salt and pepper
½ quart olive oil
1 cup vinegar
½ cup olives

1 sliced onion
2 bay leaves
2 whole cloves garlic
1 teaspoon peppercorns

Season and fry the fish in olive oil. Add the onion, bay leaves, garlic and pepper to the vinegar and cook over low heat until the onions become somewhat soft. Add the olive oil and the olives to the vinegar. Put the fish into a deep vessel of porcelain or glass and pour sauce over it. Keep it covered and it will last for several days and flavor is improved.

BREADED FRIED FISH   6 servings

3 pounds of red snapper
1½ teaspoons salt
2 tablespoons lemon juice
¼ teaspoon pepper

2 cups olive oil
4 beaten eggs
Cracker crumbs

Remove skin and bones. Slice in thick filets and season with salt,

---

[19] Any salad oil may be used instead of olive oil.

pepper and lemon juice. Put in cool place to marinate. Dip each slice in beaten egg and then cover with cracker crumbs. Fry in olive oil until brown.

CODFISH

SERENATA   6 servings

1 pound salt codfish   2 sliced tomatoes
1 sliced onion   French dressing
Olives

Soak the codfish for several hours to remove salt. Boil, remove skin and bones and cut into 1 inch pieces. Place the codfish on a serving platter and garnish with the tomato and onion slices and the olives. Pour the French dressing over the codfish. Serve with boiled vegetables: ripe and green plantain, sweet potatoes, yam, etc.

CODFISH STEW   6–8 servings
Bacalao Guisado

1½ pounds salt codfish   ½ cup tomato sauce
2 chopped peppers   1 cup water
2 chopped onions   1 pound quartered boiled pota-
1 chopped sweet pepper   toes
¼ cup olive oil   ¼ cup olives
2 cloves garlic   2 tablespoons capers

Soak codfish 2 hours in hot water. Remove bones and skin and cut into small pieces. Sauté the pepper and the onion in the oil. Add the sweet pepper, garlic, tomato sauce, water and codfish. Cook, then add the olives, capers and the potatoes. Allow to boil a while, and serve hot.

CODFISH BISCAYAN STYLE   6 servings
Bacalao a la Vizcaina

1 pound salt codfish   1 tablespoon capers
½ cup olive oil   2 cloves garlic
2 sliced onions   1 pound sliced potatoes
½ cup tomato sauce   2 baked ripe peppers
½ cup olives   ¼ cup raisins

Soak the codfish in hot water, remove skin and bones, cut into 1½

[53]

inches pieces. Put layers of codfish, onions and potatoes, tomato sauce, olives, capers and raisins, the garlic and strips of peppers. Pour the oil over the top and cook for 30 minutes over a low heat. This dish may be oven baked, if desired.

PICKLED CODFISH   8-10 servings

1½ pounds salt codfish   ½ cup vinegar
1 cup olive oil   2 bay leaves
1 sliced onion   1 teaspoon peppercorns
2 cloves garlic

Soak the codfish several hours. Remove skin and bones and cut into 2 inch pieces. Drain, dip each piece into flour and fry in oil. Sauté the onions and the garlic in the oil. Add the vinegar, bay leaves and the pepper and sauté a few minutes longer. Remove from heat and pour over the codfish.

BUCHE DE BACALAO STEW   6 servings

1 pound buche de bacalao   1 cup tomato sauce
½ cup olive oil   3 chopped pimentos
3 chopped onions   2 tablespoons capers
2 chopped green peppers   ½ cup olives

Put the codfish *buche* in water the night before. Boil, drain and cut into 1 inch pieces. Sauté the onions and the green pepper in the olive oil, and add the sauce and the *buche*. Cook over low heat. Add the pimentos, the olives and the capers and season few minutes before removing from fire.

LOBSTER AND SEA CRABS

BROILED LOBSTER   2 servings

1-3 pounds lobster   Salt and pepper to taste
Butter

Divide lobster lengthwise without removing shell. Remove stomach and intestines. Place the two halves on the broiler, shell down. Dot with butter and sprinkle salt and pepper to taste. Cook slowly for 40 minutes. Serve hot with melted butter.

STUFFED SEA CRABS   6 servings

6 sea crabs	1 teaspoon flour
1 clove garlic	3 leaves cilantro
4 peppercorns	2 tablespoons fat
Salt to taste	6 chopped olives
1 tablespoon vinegar	1 chopped tomato
1 teaspoon capers	1 chopped pepper
1 tablespoon achote coloring	1 chopped onion
½ sprig parsley	1 beaten egg

Boil the crabs, remove the legs and claws and take out the meat·
Wash and clean the shells. Grind[20] the garlic, peppercorns and salt and add the vinegar. Sauté the tomato, pepper and the onion; add the parsley and the cilantro and then the crab meat, olives and capers. Cook for several minutes over low heat. Stuff the shells. Mix the flour and the egg and cover the filling. Fry or bake for a few minutes until egg becomes firm.

LAND CRABS IN THE SHELL

Follow directions for Sea-Crabs.

EGGS AND CHEESE DISHES

Eggs and cheese are important protein foods. Because of its nutritive value they can be served as a main dish and thus add variety to the menu.

Eggs are popular and they may be used at any meal. They are easy to prepare as egg dishes do not require long cooking.

Cheese is a concentrated food easy to keep and has many uses; as a main dish, with desserts or in combination with other foods to enhance its flavor. Many of the cheeses used in cookery comes from European countries where cheese is an important item in the national diet.

---

[20] Ingredients may be pounded in a wooden mortar.

EGG DISHES

EGGS AND POTATO STEW
6 servings
Huevos Guisados con Papas

1½ pounds peeled quartered
potatoes
¼ pound chopped ham
1 sliced onion
½ cup tomato sauce
2 cups water
6 hard cooked eggs

1 chopped pepper
1 chopped clove garlic
4 tablespoons olive oil
1 teaspoon vinegar
1 tablespoon salt

Sauté the ham, onion, garlic, oil, vinegar, add the salt, pepper and tomato sauce. Add the potatoes and cook over a low heat. Cut the eggs in halves, add to the potatoes in the stew, and stir carefully. Cook all together a few minutes.

EGGS, MALAGA STYLE
6 servings
Huevos a la Malagueña

6 eggs
1 teaspoon salt
1 cup green peas

3 slices ham or 3 sausages
1 cup tomato sauce

Grease individual baking dishes. Put an egg in each one and sprinkle with salt. Cover each egg with the peas and tomato sauce and place on top strips of ham or slices of sausages. Bake in a moderate oven for several minutes or in a covered frying pan over low heat, with live charcoal on lid.

EGGS, FLEMISH STYLE
6 servings
Huevos a la Flamenca

1 chopped onion
1 chopped tomato
2 tablespoons fat
6 stalks asparagus, cut into
1½" strips
6 chopped green peppers

6 eggs
½ cup tomato sauce
½ cup peas
1 pimento cut into 1½" strips
Salt to taste

Sauté the onion, pepper and tomato. Add the asparagus. Turn into a shallow baking dish and put the eggs in the sauce. Garnish top with

[56]

a little tomato sauce, peas and strips of pimento. Bake in a moderate oven until eggs are firm. A frying pan may be used as for Eggs, Málaga Style

SCRAMBLED EGGS WITH CODFISH   6–8 servings

½ pound salt codfish   2 chopped onions
3 tablespoons fat   1 chopped green pepper
3 chopped tomatoes   6 beaten eggs

Soak the codfish a while to remove salt. Cut up in small pieces. Sauté the vegetables and add the codfish. Stir well together and add the eggs. Cook over low heat, stirring until the eggs are firm.

ONION AND BACON OMELET   6 servings

1 pound sliced onion   1 teaspoon salt
4 slices bacon   2 tablespoons fat
6 eggs

Fry bacon; remove it and sauté the onion in the same fat. Beat egg yolks, then beat whites until stiff. Mix and add the onion and bacon. Turn into a frying pan, with hot fat. Cook over low heat until eggs are firm and bottom gets brown. Turn on other side to brown.

RIPE PLANTAIN OMELET   6 servings
Tortilla de Amarillo

2 ripe plantains   1 teaspoon salt
6 eggs   Fat for frying

Peel and cut plantain into one half inch crosswise slices and sauté. Drain. Beat eggs and salt together. Turn mixture into a greased frying pan, add plantain and cook slowly until set. Cover frying pan with a lid and invert contents onto the lid. Put about a teaspoonful more fat in the frying pan and slip the omelet back into the frying pan and cook for a few minutes. Serve hot.

RIPE FINGER BANANAS AND   6 servings
STRING BEANS OMELET

Follow directions for Ripe Plantain Omelet and substitute the ripe plantains for 6 sliced finger bananas and ½ pound boiled string beans.

[57]

POTATO OMELET
Tortilla de Papas

6 servings

2 pounds potatoes
¼ pound chopped boiled ham
1 chopped Spanish sausage
6 eggs
1 onion sliced

1 cup green peas
1 tablespoon salt
1 sliced pimento
Fat for frying

Slice the potatoes thin. Fry in hot fat but do not brown. Grease a deep baking-dish. Put a layer of potatoes garnished with small pieces of ham, sausage, peas and onion. Sprinkle with salt. Repeat until ingredients are used. Arrange the pimento strips on top spreading out like sun rays. Between the strips of pimento put the eggs. Bake in moderate oven until the eggs are firm.

POTATO AND SPANISH SAUSAGE OMELET
Tortilla de Papas y Chorizo

6 servings

2 pounds potatoes
¼ pound minced onions
2 chopped Spanish sausages

6 beaten egg yolks
6 beaten whites, stiff
½ teaspoon salt
Fat for frying

Slice the potatoes in thin slices and put into salted water. Drain and fry in hot fat. Stir constantly while frying, so slices are cooked and have a light brown color. Sauté the onion. Mix together the onion, potatoes and sausages. Add whites to egg yolks, add the salt and add the potato mixture. Stir together well. Put into a frying pan with hot fat and cook over low heat. Turn to brown other side.

HAM OMELET

6 servings

½ pound chopped ham
¼ pound chopped onion
1 chopped green pepper
1 teaspoon salt

4 chopped tomatoes
6 beaten egg yolks
6 beaten whites, stiff

Sauté the ham, onion, pepper and tomatoes. Add egg whites to egg yolks and turn into a greased skillet. Place over a low heat and as soon as eggs begin to set add the filling. Fold the omelet over to cover the filling. Serve either with or without tomato sauce on top.

BRAIN OMELET   6 servings

1 brain	4 tablespoons fat
1 quart water	⅛ teaspoon pepper
1 teaspoon salt	2 tablespoons minced parsley
6 eggs	1 teaspoon salt

Boil the brain 15 minutes. Allow to cool, remove all dark tissues and mash well. Fold whites into the egg yolk mixture, add the brain, pepper, parsley and salt. Fry in a large frying-pan over moderate heat. As soon as bottom is brown, turn omelet over and brown the other side.

CHEESE DISHES

STUFFED CHEESE   12 servings

1 Edam cheese	1 minced clove garlic
1–2 pounds chicken	½ cup tomato sauce
½ cup olives	1½ teaspoons salt
¼ cup raisins	3 chopped hard cooked eggs
4 tablespoons olive oil	

Make a square incision in the top of the cheese and remove square piece of rind to be used later as the top. Remove cheese with a teaspoon, taking care not to break rind.[21] Soak rind and square piece for several hours to soften it. If it is very hard put it in hot water. Cut up the chicken, season and make a fricassee with the chicken, olives, raisins, onion, oil, garlic, tomato sauce and the salt. When the chicken is tender remove the bones and mix the meat with the chopped eggs. Stuff the cheese with the chicken and put the top of the cheese in place.[22] Grease the outside of cheese all around. Put a plantain leaf in the bottom of a kettle. Place cheese shell on leaf and cook over a low heat. If desired, the cheese may be baked in a moderate oven.

---

[21] Cheese removed may be used for other cheese dishes.

[22] The cheese shell may be stuffed with pork meat, with spaghetti or with spaghetti cooked with squab.

CHAYOTE STUFFED WITH CHEESE   8 servings

4 chayotes   ½ teaspoon pepper
2 teaspoons salt   2 beaten eggs
1 cup grated Edam cheese   ½ cup cracker crumbs

Cut the chayotes in halves lengthwise. Steam or boil until pulp is
soft. Remove pulp but do not break rind or shells. Mash the pulp
with a fork, add the salt, cheese and pepper. Mix well and stuff shells.
Beat the eggs and spread on top to cover the chayote. Sprinkle with
cracker crumbs. Cook in a moderate oven 350° F for 20 minutes.

BAKED EGGPLANT WITH CHEESE   6 servings

2 pounds eggplant   1 teaspoon salt
½ cup olive oil   1 cup chopped tomatoes
2 chopped onions   2 tablespoons olive oil
2 cloves garlic   ¼ pound Parmesan cheese

Slice the eggplant without peeling. Sprinkle with salt and sauté in
the olive oil. Sauté the onions, garlic and tomatoes in the two tablespoonfuls olive oil. Grease a baking-dish and arrange a layer of sliced
eggplant, another of grated cheese and pour over part of the sauce.
Repeat until dish is full. Sprinkle with grated cheese. Cook in moderate oven or in a kettle over low heat for 45 minutes.

For other fish recipes please see Chapters VI and VIII and for
cheese recipes see Chapter VI.

FRIED FOODS

Frying is one of the most popular methods of preparing foods. Some kind of fried food or "fritura" is included very often in the menu; many foods such as "pastelillos", "tostones", etc., develop a delicious flavor when fried.

For deep fat frying about two pounds of fat or a quart of oil are needed for a medium-size kettle or pan. A relatively small amount of fat is absorbed by food during a single frying. After each use cool and strain fat and store in refrigerator. For pan frying put enough fat to a depth of 1½″ in the pan. There will be less fat left over. The best fats for frying are those fats which will not smoke at a high temperature.

The essential equipment for deep fat frying is a heavy saucepan about 2 quarts size and a frying basket and slotted or perforated metal spoon; for pan frying a heavy skillet about 8″ in diameter and a pancake turner or slotted spoon are needed.

Deep Fat Frying Chart

	Temp. F.	Minutes
Croquettes (cooked foods)	375–390	2–5
"Almojábanas", "pastelillos"!	360–370	2–3
Fish	390	5–10
Chicken or rabbit	375–390	25–30
Pork chops or breaded cutlets	375–400	10–15
Sliced plantains and sweet potatoes	395	4–6

TOSTÓNES   15 tostones

3 plantains   Water
2 teaspoons salt   Fat for frying

Peel the plantains. Cut crosswise in slices about ½ inch wide. Slant the knife while cutting so slices will have an oval shape. Place in ·alted water for one hour. Drain. Fry until plantain is tender, but

[61]

not crusty. Remove from fat, flatten by pressing evenly, dip in salted water and fry again until crusty. Drain on absorbent paper.

PLANTAIN CHIPS
Platanutri

8 servings

3 plantains	Fat for frying
Salt	

Peel the plantains. Slice very fine and place in iced water for ½ hour. Drain and dry. Fry in deep fat until crispy. Remove from fat and drain; then place in paper bag, sprinkle salt and shake to distribute salt evenly.

MOFONGO

6 servings

4 plantains	Fat for frying
½ pound pork crackling	

Cut plantains as for tostones and fry. Grind tostones in a mortar, add crackling a little at a time, grind and mix well. Shape into balls and serve hot.

ALCAPURRIAS

6 servings

3 green plantains	1 tablespoon salt
1 pound white yautía	2 cups meat filling
Fat for frying	

Peel the plantains and the yautías and put them into salted water. Grate them on the finest side of the grater and add the salt. Spread two tablespoons of mixture over a piece of plantain leaf or waxed paper, place two teaspoonfuls of filling in the center and fold leaf to shape as a fried pie. Fry in hot fat until light brown. Drain.

FRIED RIPE PLANTAIN

6 servings

3 ripe plantains	Fat for frying

Peel plantains. Cut in halves and slice lengthwise into 4 or 5 slices each. Fry until tender and golden brown. Drain.

FRIED RIPE FINGER BANANAS
AND GRATED CHEESE
Guineitos Fritos con Queso

6 servings

18 ripe finger bananas
½ cup grated native or Edam
cheese

Fat for frying

Peel and fry bananas until golden brown. Drain on absorbent paper.
Place on platter and sprinkle generously with grated cheese. Serve
hot.

RIPE PLANTAIN IN SYRUP
Plátanos Maduros al Sartén

6 servings

3 ripe plantains[1]
4 tablespoons fat
2¼ cups hot water

3 tablespoons butter
¾ cup sugar
2 sticks cinnamon

Peel plantains. Fry slowly until golden brown. Drain. Mix water,
butter, sugar and cinnamon; and add plantains. Cook slowly until
plantains are done.

PIONONOS

6 servings

3 ripe plantains
1½ cups meat filling
2 beaten eggs

¼ teaspoon salt
Fat for frying

Peel the plantains, slice lengthwise into 4 or 5 slices each and fry them
until tender. Drain on absorbent paper. Shape each slice into a circle
and fasten edges with a tooth pick. Fill each circle with filling. Cover
open ends with beaten egg and fry in hot fat.

NOTE: Instead of beaten egg, a stiff mixture of flour and water
may be used to cover ends.

PIÑÓN

8 servings

4 ripe plantains
1 pound cooked string beans
¼ cup fat

2 cups meat filling
6 eggs
½ teaspoon salt

Peel and slice the ripe plantains lengthwise and fry them. Cut the

---

[1] Plantains must be very ripe, the skin almost black.

[63]

string beans into 1 inch lengths and mix them with the filling. Beat the eggs and add the salt. Heat the fat in the frying pan and pour half the beaten eggs into it. Cover with half the slices of ripe plantain. Spread all the meat filling over the slices and cover with remaining slices of plantain. By this time the egg will be firm. Cover frying pan with a lid and invert contents on the lid. Put a bit more fat in the frying pan and pour the rest of the beaten egg. Slip the piñón back into the frying pan and cook for few minutes for egg on bottom to thicken.

NOTE: The piñón may be baked. When the remaining slices of ripe plantain are placed over the filling, pour the rest of the beaten egg over and bake in a moderate oven 350° for 15 or 20 minutes or until the egg is done.

FRIED SWEET POTATO   6 servings

1½ pounds sweet potato   Fat for frying

Peel sweet potato, preferable the yellow variety (mameya). Cut into slices ½ inch thick. Place in salted water for one half hour. Drain. Fry in deep fat. Drain on absorbent paper.

FRIED EGGPLANT   4 servings

1 pound eggplant   1 teaspoon baking powder
1 cup milk   ¾ teaspoon salt
1 cup flour   Fat for frying

Slice eggplants crosswise, ¼ of an inch thick. Mix flour, salt and baking powder, add milk to make a batter. Dip slices in batter and fry slowly until golden brown. Drain and sprinkle with sugar if desired.

BREADFRUIT CHIPS   8 servings
Hojuelas de Panapén

1 breadfruit   Fat for frying
Salt

Peel breadfruit. Cut in quarters, discard central spongy section. Slice each quarter very fine. Place in boiling water for one minute. Remove from water and drain well. Fry in deep fat until golden brown and crisp. Drain. Sprinkle with salt and stir to distribute salt evenly.

BREADFRUIT FRITTERS
Tortitas de Panapén

8 fritters

2 cups mashed boiled bread-
    fruit
2 tablespoons butter
½ teaspoon salt

2 tablespoons grated cheese
1 beaten egg
Fat for frying

Add salt and butter to breadfruit and mix well. Add egg and cheese.
Shape like little round cakes 2½ inches by ¼ of an inch and fry.
Drain.

PUMPKIN FRITTERS
Frituras de Calabaza

16 fritters

2 cups mashed boiled pump-
    kin
½ cup flour
1 teaspoon salt
2 beaten eggs

¼ teaspoon cloves
½ teaspoon cinnamon
2 tablespoons sugar
Fat for frying

Mix and sift together flour, salt, cloves, cinnamon and sugar. Add
flour and beaten eggs to pumpkin and stir to blend well. Drop by
spoonfuls and pan-fry. Drain.

GREEN CORN FRITTERS

16 fritters

¾ cup flour
¼ teaspoon salt
½ teaspoon baking powder
¼ teaspoon cinnamon

1 cup grated green corn
1 beaten egg
Fat for frying

Mix the dry ingredients and add to the corn. Add beaten egg and mix
well. Drop by teaspoonfuls, and fry in deep fat. Sprinkle with sugar
before serving.

YUCA AND GREEN CORN FRITTERS

12 fritters

1 cup grated green corn
¾ cup yuca flour
½ teaspoon baking powder

¼ teaspoon cinnamon
1 beaten egg
Fat for frying

Mix the yuca flour, baking powder, and cinnamon, add to the green corn and mix well. Add beaten egg. Drop by teaspoonfuls into deep fat. Drain on absorbent paper.

YAM FRITTERS   16 fritters

1 pound grated yam   2 beaten eggs
1½ teaspoons salt   3 tablespoons flour
                            Fat for frying

Mix all ingredients. Drop by teaspoonfuls into deep fat and fry as Apio Cruller.

BRAIN FRITTERS   12–16 fritters

1 boiled brain   1½ cups flour
1½ cups milk   Fat for frying
1 teaspoon salt

Cut brain in slices, ½ inch thick. Mix flour and salt and add milk to make a batter. Dip slices in batter and pan fry. Drain. Serve hot with lemon slices.

SHRIMP FRITTERS   12–16 fritters

1 pound shrimps   ½ teaspoon baking powder
1 cup flour   ½ teaspoon salt
1 cup milk   Fat for frying

Place shrimps in saucepan, add enough water to cover, add salt and cover tightly. Boil for 20 minutes. Clean shrimps by cutting thin shell with a pointed knife, remove tail, and black line that lies close to the surface. Mix salt, flour, baking powder and milk. Dip shrimps in batter and fry in deep fat. Drain.

BACALAITOS   24 bacalaitos

½ pound salted codfish   ½ teaspoon baking powder
2 cups flour   2 ground cloves garlic
2 cups water   Fat for frying
½ teaspoon salt

Soak the codfish for two hours to remove part of the salt. Remove bones and skin and cut into small pieces. Mix flour and baking powder and add the codfish, garlic and water. Mix well, and if necessary add salt. Drop by teaspoonfuls and fry in deep fat. Drain on absorbent paper.

BACALAITOS IN SAUCE

4 tablespoons olive oil	1 cup tomato sauce
2 diced onions	$\frac{1}{2}$ cup water
1 sprig parsley	

Fry the onion in olive oil. Mince the parsley and add to the onion. Add the tomato sauce and water and boil for few minutes. Pour over the Bacalaitos.

ALMOJÁBANAS   36 crullers
Rice Meal Cruller

$\frac{1}{2}$ cup flour	4 tablespoons melted butter
$\frac{1}{4}$ cup water	1 cup grated native cheese
1 cup rice meal	$\frac{1}{4}$ cup grated Parmesan or
2 teaspoons baking powder	Edam cheese
Salt to taste	Fat for frying
4 eggs	

Add the water to the flour and let stand for two or three hours before preparing the cruller. Mix the rice meal with the baking powder and salt and add to the flour mixture. Add one egg at a time and beat vigorously for a few minutes. Add the melted butter and cheese. Add enough milk, to make a thick batter[2]. Drop by teaspoonfuls and fry in deep fat until golden brown. Drain on absorbent paper. See illust.

APIO CRULLER   16 crullers
Buñuelos de Apio

1 pound apio	1 teaspoon salt
3 beaten eggs	Fat for frying

Boil and mash the apio. Add eggs and salt, mix well. Drop by teaspoonfuls into deep fat and fry until brown and cooked in the center (4 to 5 minutes). Drain on absorbent paper.

---

[2] The amount of milk needed depends upon the size of the eggs, and the absorbing power of the flour. If large eggs are used, less milk is needed.

[67]

YAM AND CHEESE CRULLER

20 crullers

2 cups grated yam
½ cup flour
2 tablespoons fat
1 teaspoon salt

3 tablespoons grated native
cheese
1 beaten egg
6 tablespoons milk
Fat for frying

Mix all ingredients. Drop by teaspoonfuls into deep fat and fry until brown and well cooked in the center. Drain. Sprinkle with sugar or serve with guava jelly.

SURULLITOS

10 surullitos

1½ cups cornmeal
½ teaspoon salt
1¼ cups hot water

⅓ cup grated native cheese
Fat for frying

Mix cornmeal and salt and add the water. Cook for few minutes until thick like mush. Add cheese and let cool. Shape the surullitos into cylinders about ¾" wide and 3" or 3½" long. Pan-fry and drain on absorbent paper. See illustration.

CORNMEAL CAKES
Arepitas

12–14 arepitas

1 cup cornmeal
4 cups water

1 teaspoon salt
1 cup grated native cheese
Fat for frying

Boil the water, add salt and cornmeal. Stir constantly until mixture gets thick. Add the cheese and let cool. Shape into round cakes, about 2½ inches in diameter and ½" thick. Pan-fry and drain.

CORNMEAL AND CHEESE CRULLER
Buñuelos de Maíz y Queso

20 crullers

1½ quarts milk
¾ teaspoon salt
2 cups cornmeal

1 cup grated native cheese
4 eggs
Fat for frying

Heat the milk, add salt then cornmeal slowly, stirring to prevent lumps. Cook in low heat and stir constantly until the cornmeal gets thick and tastes done. Remove from heat and let cool. Add the eggs, one at a time, beating vigorously after each addition. Drop by teaspoonfuls into deep fat. Fry until golden brown. Drain on absorbent paper.

CORNMEAL TURNOVERS   8 turnovers

2 cups cornmeal	1 pepper
4 cups water	1 tomato
1 teaspoon salt	1 teaspoon salt
1 pound pork meat	2 tablespoons fat
1 onion	Fat for frying
2 ounces smoked ham	

Cook the cornmeal as for cornmeal cakes. Grind pork, ham and vegetables in the meat grinder. Add salt and cook in fat until pork is tender. Take a piece of plantain leaf about 8″ square. Spread two tablespoons cornmeal mush on greased leaf or paper to form a circle about 4″ in diameter. Put one tablespoon meat on one side, fold over leaf to shape the turnover. Press the edges and slip carefully from leaf into pan and fry on both sides. Drain. See illustration

PORK TURNOVERS   36 turnovers

Pastry

4 cups flour	1 beaten egg
2 teaspoons salt	Cold water or milk
4 tablespoons fat	Fat for frying

Sift together flour and salt. Add the fat, cutting it into the flour with two knives or a dough blender until the flour has the consistency of very coarse meal. Mix the egg with ½ cup water and add to the flour, sprinkling a little at a time in the center. Stir from edges toward center. When sufficient water has been added and the dough is compact and soft, shape into several small balls, cover with waxed paper and keep in the refrigerator until ready to use. See illustration.

Filling

1 pound pork meat	1 teaspoon salt
2 ounces smoked ham	2 tablespoons fat
1 ounce salt pork	$\frac{1}{3}$ cup pitted olives
2 tomatoes	1 tablespoon capers
1 pepper	$\frac{1}{4}$ cup raisins
1 onion	2 hard boiled eggs

Grind pork, ham, salt pork and vegetables. Add salt and cook in fat until pork is tender. Add olives, raisins and capers, chop eggs and add to pork before removing from heat.

To shape turnover: Take a small ball of pastry and flatten slightly by pressing with floured rolling pin; then roll lightly from center toward the edges. Turn the pastry upside down on floured board and roll again, several times until it is about $\frac{1}{8}$ inch thick or less. Cut circles 4″ in diameter. Place a tablespoon of filling on the center side; moisten edges around. Fold over, so both edges meet and press down with tines of fork. Fry in deep fat. When turnovers rise to the top, pour over fat with a spoon, so pastry will puff, turn to brown on both sides. Drain on absorbent paper.

NOTE: Turnovers are made very small about 2½″ in diameter to serve as appetizers or with cocktails and drinks. The filling may be pork or cheese: équal parts of grated native or American cheese and Parmesan or Edam cheese; guava paste or jelly may also be used.

CHEESE TURNOVERS
Pastelillos de Queso

Same recipe as "Pastelillos" (Pork Turnover). Instead of pork filling use grated cheese: White native, American or Edam cheese. To one cup American or native cheese, add about one fourth cup of grated Parmesan cheese. Use two teaspoons of grated cheese for each turnover.

SWEET POTATO CROQUETTES 10 croquettes
Croquetas de Batata

3 cups mashed sweet potatoes	¼ cup sugar
2 tablespoons butter	3 beaten eggs
1 teaspoon salt	½ teaspoon salt
2 eggs	1½ cups bread crumbs
¼ teaspoon cinnamon	Fat for frying

Add butter, salt, eggs, cinnamon and sugar to mashed sweet potato. Mix well. Shape into croquettes. Roll in bread crumbs, dip into salted beaten egg, then roll in bread crumbs again and fry in deep fat. Drain on absorbent paper. Serve hot with orange marmalade.

YAUTÍA CROQUETTES 6 croquettes

2 cups mashed yautía	½ teaspoon salt
2 tablespoons butter	2 beaten eggs
2 eggs	¼ teaspoon salt
1 tablespoon grated onion	1 cup bread crumbs
⅛ teaspoon pepper	Fat for frying

Follow directions for Sweet Potato Croquettes. Serve with guava jelly.

PORK CROQUETTES 8 croquettes

1½ pounds ground pork	2 tablespoons grated onion
1 tablespoon salt	3 beaten eggs
3 tablespoons butter	½ teaspoon salt
¼ teaspoon pepper	1½ cups bread crumbs
1½ cups milk	Fat for deep fat frying
½ cup flour	

Add salt to pork and cook at low heat until pork is done. Prepare a thick white sauce with butter, flour, milk, salt and pepper. Remove from heat. Add the onion and pork, and mix well. Cool. Divide the cool mixture in 8 parts and shape into balls or roll on a board to form cylinders. Add salt to beaten egg. Roll croquettes in crumbs, dip in beaten egg, then in crumbs. Fry in deep fat until brown, 7 to 8 minutes. Drain on absorbent paper.

[71]

FISH CROQUETTES
6 croquettes

2 cups flaked boiled snapper
1 teaspoon grated onion
1 cup thick white sauce
2 beaten eggs

¼ teaspoon salt
1½ cups bread crumbs
Fat for frying

Add onion and fish to white sauce, mix well. Shape mixture into croquettes,[3] add salt to beaten egg. Roll croquettes in crumbs in beaten eggs, then in crumbs and fry in deep fat. Drain on absorbent paper.

CHICKEN CROQUETTES
10 croquettes

1—2 pounds ready to cook
  chicken, cup up
1 quart water
½ teaspoon salt
½ cup flour
3 tablespoons butter
1 teaspoon salt

¼ teaspoon pepper
1 tablespoon grated onion
1½ cups chicken broth
3 beaten eggs
½ teaspoon salt
1½ cups bread crumbs
Fat for frying

Boil water, add salt and chicken. Cover and cook at low heat until meat is tender. Separate meat from bones and grind or cut into small pieces. Prepare a thick sauce with butter, flour, salt, pepper and chicken broth. Season to taste. Remove from heat and cool. Add the chicken and onion, mix well. Shape into croquettes. Dip in bread crumbs, then in salted beaten eggs, and again in crumbs and fry in deep fat. Drain on absorbent paper.

---

[3] See directions for Pork Croquettes.

CHAPTER VII

VEGETABLES

There is a great variety of root vegetables in Puerto Rico. Most of the vegetables are indigenous such as "yautía", "batata", "yuca" and "lerén", while others have been introduced from other countries as the "papa" and "ñame".

All the starchy roots are classified as "viandas" and there are different ways of serving them: grated are made into fritters, turnovers and meat pies; eggplant, peppers and "chayotes" are stuffed with meat or cheese; and boiled or fried are served as accompaniment to other dishes.

Following is a list of the most common vegetables found in the market at different times:

AVOCADO. Aguacate; persea persea. A very important food fruit, used for salads and to accompany meals.

APIO. Arracacha; arracacia zanthorrhiza. Root, yellow starch, strong flavor.

BANANA, GREEN. Guineo verde; musa sapientum. The green banana is used as a vegetable, consumed widely especially in the rural areas.

BREADFRUIT, SEED. Pana de pepita; artocarpus communis. Seed resembles chestnuts, good flavor, generally eaten boiled.

BREADFRUIT, SEEDLESS. Pana, panapen; artocarpus incisa. Yellow fine pulp; cheap, may substitute potato.

CASSAVA. Yuca; manihot manihot. There are two types: the sweet (dulce) and the bitter (brava). There is no botanical distinction between the two. The sweet cassava is found in the market almost the year round.

CHAYOTE. Tallote; sechim edule. Two varieties: the green and the white skin. Found in the market almost year round.

CORN, SWEET. Maíz tierno; zea mays. Best variety of sweet corn is the USDA No. 34; now grown all over the island.

EGGPLANT. Berenjena; solanum melongena. The most common and best varieties are: Rosita, light purple, "Striped"

[73]

LEREN. Sweet corn root; calathea allovia. Root vegetable; develops the flavor of sweet corn when boiled.

LETTUCE. Lechuga; lactuca sativa. A leaf lettuce salad plant, leaves must be carefully washed before using.

OKRA. Guingambó; abelmoschus esculentus. Pods slightly round, smooth surface.

PEPPER. Pimiento; capsicum annum. There are several varieties, the long fruit, thin skin; the short, thick skin suitable for stuffing and salads. (P. R. Wonder or California Wonder).

PEPPER, SWEET. Ají dulce; capsicum annuum. Fruit small, flat round has a mild, sweet flavor. Much used for seasoning meats, soups, etc.

PEPPER, DEVIL. Ají caballero; capsicum annuum. Minute fruits, conical shape extremely pungent. The ripe fruit is a dark red.

PEPPER, CAYENNE. Ají bravo; capsicum annuum. Long red fruits, curved at the tip.

PLANTAIN. Plátano; musa paradisiaca. Very popular vegetable and very nutritive; eaten in the green and ripe stage (amarillos). There are several varieties: *Congo*, large plant, not so abundant, few plantations. *Enano*, small plant, excellent quality.

SQUASH. Calabaza; pepo moschata. Field pumpkin type.

SWEET POTATO. Batata; ipomaea batata. Best variety is the "mameya", a deep yellow and sweeter taste, richer in vitamin A. "White", white skin and starch, and "red", red skinned and white starch.

SWISS CHARD. Acelga; beta vulgaris. A common green, found at the market and used for soups and other dishes.

WATER CRESS. Berros; sysymbrium nasturtium aquaticum. Very common salad plant.

YAUTÍA, WHITE. Yautía blanca; zanthosoma caracu. Best variety, white starch, softer when cooked.

YAUTÍA, PURPLE. Medium large, reddish purple starch.

YAUTÍA, YELLOW. Yautía amarilla; zanthosoma sagitaefolium. Yellow starch, when cooked remains quite hard and should be eaten while hot.

YAM, WATER. Ñame de agua; dioscorea alata. The starch is snow white. Shape of the roots very irregular.

YAM, GUINEA. Ñame guinea; habanero; portugués; dioscorea rotundata. The best of the common yams, the roots are nearly cylindrical, peel corky if mature; smooth, also yellow or white color starch.

YAM, FLORIDA. Resembles white yam, dark skin, round shape and long.

YAMPEE. Ñame mapuey; dioscorea trifida. Smallest of the yams; and most expensive; two varieites, the white (blanco) has white starch and the purple (morado) has a purplish starch. Fine flavor.

Our succulent vegetables may be classified as follows: Greens and yellows: includes all dark green leaves such as swiss chard, and the tender leaves of turnips and beets. The yellow ones include pumpkin, carrots, and yellow sweet potato (batata mameya). All these vegetables are rich in vitamin A; the greens also provide other vitamins besides iron salts. String beans, okra, cabbage, tomato, and green pigeon-peas are not as rich in vitamins and mineral salts as the first group.

Eggplant, chayote, beets, and green corn have little food value, but they are combined with other foods to increase their nutritive value; they also help to add variety to our meals.

The salad group includes lettuce, water cress, cucumber and radish. They are eaten in such small quantities that their contribution in vitamins and mineral salts is not so important, but they also add variety.

There are some cooking herbs, seeds and roots used as aromatic condiments to improve the flavor of many dishes.

ANISE SEED. Anis; pimpinella anisum. Seeds and leaves are used for stews and sauces.

BAY LEAF. Hoja de laurel. The aromatic leaves of the sweet-bay, one of the fragrant species of the laurel family.

CORIANDER. Cilantro; coriandrum sativum. Has long, serrated leaves, seeds are also used for seasoning.

CORIANDER, WILD. Cilantro del monte; eryngium faetidum. A very common seasoning herb grows wild in fields and along road sides.

GARLIC. Ajo, allium sativum. One of the most common condiments, usually pounded in a mortar with salt, and marjoram to season meats and poultry.

GINGER. Jengibre, zingiber zingiber. Spiced root extensively used in cooking to flavor desserts, drinks and other dishes.

MARJORAM, POT. Orégano; origanum vulgare. A very popular seasoning herb with small, oval, dark green leaves.

MARJORAM, ORIENTAL. Orégano brujo; coleus amboinicus. A common garden herb, has thick juicy stems and leaves.

[75]

MINT. Hierbabuena; mentha citrata. Garden mint; common seasoning herb.

PARSLEY. Perejil; apium petroselinum. A savory·herb very much used for seasoning meats.

BOILED

BOILED VEGETABLES

Viandas Hervidas

Peel and cook in boiling salted water. Add enough water to cover them. Cut and serve hot, with olive oil or butter. Boiled vegetables are served with meats, fish and codfish.

MASHED YAM   6 servings

2 pounds yam	2 teaspoons salt
4 tablespoons butter	1 cup hot milk

Peel yam. Heat water, add salt, and boil yam. Mash yam, add butter and beat in hot milk to make it fluffy. Add more salt if necessary. Keep hot until ready to serve.

MASHED YAUTIA, SWEET POTATO OR BRFADFRUIT

Follow directions for Mashed Yam. Yautia and sweet potato requires longer cooking and more milk. Breadfruit must be underripe, if mature it is not mealy and develops a sweet taste.

BAKED

BAKED GREEN PLANTAIN·

Peel plantain, wrap in a buttered piece of brown paper. Bake in a moderate oven for about 1 hour or until tender. Remove from paper and serve hot.

BAKED RIPE PLANTAIN

Cut ends of ripe plantain. Place on rack and bake in moderate oven for about 1 hour. It is done when peeling bursts. Remove peeling, butter and place again in the oven to brown.

GLAZED SWEET POTATO   6 servings

   2 pounds boiled sweet potato   4 tablespoons butter
   ½ cup brown sugar

Slice sweet potato. Place slices in greased baking pan, and dot with butter. Sprinkle sugar. Bake in moderate oven until sugar turns into caramel.

CASABE   4 cakes

   1 pound cassava   Salt to taste

Wash and peel the cassava. Grate in a grater using the finest section. Squeeze to remove all the water possible. Heat a frying pan. Shape the casabe into a cake, quite thin and bake until golden brown on both sides.

STEWED

STRING BEAN STEW   6 servings

   1½ pounds string beans   1 cup water
   ½ cup sofrito   2 tablespoons olives
   1 teaspoon salt   ½ teaspoon capers

Wash and remove stem and ends from string beans. Cut in halves and mix with the sofrito. Add water and salt and cook at low heat until tender.

OKRA STEW   6 servings

   1½ pounds okra   1 teaspoon salt
   ½ cup sofrito   ½ cup stock

Wash okra, and cut in pieces about 1 inch. Mix okra with sofrito. Add stock and cook at low heat uncovered until tender.

EGGPLANT STEW   6 servings

   ¼ pound smoked ham   2 pounds eggplant cut into 1″
   2 tomatoes   cubes
   2 green peppers   1 tablespoon salt
   2 onions   ¼ cup water
   2 tablespoons fat

Cut ham and vegetables in small pieces, and fry lightly. Add water and eggplant. Add salt to taste. Stir. Cook at a low heat for about twenty minutes.

EGGPLANT STEW WITH PORK   8 servings

Follow directions for Eggplant Stew. Add one pound pork cut in $\frac{3}{4}$ inch cubes. Cook the meat and vegetables a little longer and add more salt to taste.

SWISS CHARD STEW   6 servings

3 bunches chard   1 diced onion
$\frac{1}{4}$ cup water   1 diced pepper
1 teaspoon salt   2 ounces smoked ham
2 diced tomatoes   1 tablespoon fat

Wash chard and cut stems and leaves in small pieces about 2 inches long. Cut ham in cubes and fry with vegetables, add chard and salt. Cook at low heat for few minutes. When stems are tender it is ready to serve.

NOTE: You may add 3 beaten eggs before serving. Any left over ground meat or native sausage may be added instead of eggs. The vegetable stews may be served with Boiled "Viandas" or Boiled Rice.

ALBORONÍA DE CHAYOTE   6 servings

3 chayotes   6 eggs
1 cup sofrito $\frac{1}{2}$ teaspoon salt
$\frac{1}{2}$ cup water

Peel and cut chayotes into 1" cubes. Add sofrito, salt and water to the chayote, and cook slowly until chayote is tender and most of the water has evaporated. Beat the eggs and add to chayote. Cook at a very low heat, and stir until eggs are firm. Serve hot.

CREAMED CHAYOTE   8 servings

4 chayotes   1 teaspoon salt
4 tablespoons corn starch   2 tablespoons raisins
$\frac{3}{4}$ cup sugar   2 tablespoons melted butter
2 egg yolks $\frac{1}{2}$ cup cracker crumbs
1 cup milk

Cut chayotes lengthwise. Place chayotes in pan, and add enough boiling water to cover, add salt and cook until tender. Remove the

[78]

pulp carefully, discarding central section, and save shell for refilling. Mash pulp. Beat egg yolks with sugar and add salt, conrstarch, milk, chayotes and butter. Cook at low heat or in double boiler stirring to prevent lumping. When mixture is thick remove from heat and refill the shells. Sprinkle top with cracker crumbs.

STUFFED VEGETABLES

MEAT FILLING   **2 cups**

1 pound pork meat	1 ounce onion
2 ounces ground ham	2 tablespoons lard
1 ounce ground salt pork	Salt to taste
1 ounce green pepper	2 tablespoons olives
2 ounces tomato	1 tablespoon capers

Grind together the pork, ham, salt pork, pepper, tomato and onion, or if you wish, mince them fine with a knife. Sauté mixture with lard at low heat until the meat is cooked. Season to taste and add the olives and capers.

STUFFED POTATOES   **8–10 servings**

1½ pounds potatoes	2 cups meat filling
1 tablespoon salt	1 beaten egg
4 tablespoons flour	Fat for frying

Boil and mash the potatoes. Add the salt, egg and flour and mix well. Divide into 8 or 10 equal parts. Flour the hands and take one part and spread it over the palm in circular form. Place a tablespoon of the filling in the center and bring up edges to cover filling and form a ball. If desired the stuffed potato may be given a cylindrical shape. Fry in hot fat.

STUFFED BREADFRUIT

Follow directions for Stuffed Potatoes.

STUFFED PEPPERS   **6 servings**

6 large green peppers	¼ teaspoon salt
1½ cups meat filling	Fat for frying
1 beaten egg	

Cut upper part of pepper about ½″ from stem and remove seeds.

Dip in boiling water and parboil for two minutes. Stuff the peppers and cover tops with beaten eggs. Fry them or bake at 350°F for 15 or 20 minutes.

STUFFED RIPE PLANTAIN   6 servings

3 ripe plantains $1\frac{1}{2}$ cups meat filling
1 teaspoon salt   Fat for frying
6 tablespoons flour

Boil plantains in salted water. When tender, peel, mash and divide into 6 portions. Flour the hand and spread one portion over the palm in circular form. Put a tablespoon of filling in the center, bring up edges together to cover filling and shape into a ball. Fry in hot fat.

STUFFED EGGPLANT   8 servings

4 eggplants   2 beaten eggs
2 cups meat filling $\frac{1}{4}$ teaspoon salt
2 tablespoons flour   Fat for frying

Cut the eggplants in two lengthwise, and boil until tender. Remove pulp without breaking the shell and mix with the filling. Stuff the eggplant shells. Mix the egg, flour and salt and cover them. Fry in hot fat or bake at 350°F until egg is cooked.

STUFFED CHAYOTES   8 servings

4 chayotes, (large) $\frac{1}{4}$ teaspoon salt
$1\frac{1}{2}$ cups meat filling   Fat for frying
2 beaten eggs

Wash and cut the chayotes in halves lengthwise. Boil until pulp is soft. Remove pulp with teaspoon without breaking shells. Mash the pulp with a fork and mix with the filling. Fill the shells. Beat the eggs, season with salt and cover the chayotes. Fry them in hot fat or bake like Stuffed Eggplant.

STUFFED ONIONS   8 servings

2 large onions   1 beaten egg
2 cups meat filling   Fat for frying
$\frac{1}{8}$ teaspoon salt

Cut off about $\frac{1}{4}''$ slices from top and bottom of onions and boil until slightly cooked. Remove from water and allow to cool. Separate the shells by pushing from lower bottom and removing the center. Be careful not to break the layers. Stuff each shell with filling, and cover each end with egg so that the filling will not drop out. Fry in hot lard or bake.

PLANTAIN PASTELES   12 pasteles

3 green plantains[1]
½ pound white yautia
1 cup milk[2]
1 tablespoon salt
½ cup achote coloring
1 pound pork meat
¼ pound ham
¼ tablespoon salt
¼ pound salt pork
2 tablespoons capers
½ cup olives
⅓ cup raisins
1 cup cooked chick peas

1 chopped onion
1 chopped green pepper
2 chopped tomatoes
2 chopped sweet peppers
3 cilantro leaves, minced
1 minced sprig cilantrillo
¼ cup achote coloring
½ teaspoon powdered marjoram
½ cup water
3 packages plantain leaf
String to tie

Peel the plantain and the yautía and soak in salted water for 5 minutes. Grate vegetables on the finest side of the grater. Add the milk, and salt, and achote coloring; mix well so that color will be uniform throughout. Season to taste and set aside until filling is made. Chop the pork, ham, salt pork into small pieces and add the capers, olives, raisins, chick peas, onion, pepper, tomatoes, sweet peppers, cilantro, cilantrillo, achote coloring and orégano. Add ½ cup of water and cook for 20 minutes. Clean and trim the plantain leaves and cut into 10 inch pieces. Use one or two pieces for each pastel. Grease each leaf and put about ⅓ cup vegetable mixture in center of leaf, spread it out to a rectangular shape.[3] Place about 2 tablespoons of filling along one side. Fold the leaf lengthwise so edges of mixture meet, turn sides toward middle, and turn ends down. Place two pasteles together with folded sides inside, tie and boil for 45 minutes in salted water. Remove from water and drain before serving. Serve hot.

---

[1] Green bananas are also used.
[2] Liquid obtained from the meat filling may be used.
[3] See illustration.

RICE PASTELES

6 pasteles

2 cups rice
2 teaspoons salt

4 tablespoons achote coloring

Wash the rice and add the salt and achote coloring, a little of the sauce from the filling may be used. Follow the directions given for making the plantain pasteles. Spread the rice as the vegetable mixture and boil in salted water for 1 hour. Remove from water and drain before serving. Serve hot.

EMPANADA DE APIO

8 empanadas

4 cups grated apio
Salt to taste
¼ cup achote coloring

2 cups meat filling
1 package plantain leaves
Melted fat

Season the grated apio, add achote coloring and mix well. Clean and trim the plantain leaf and cut into pieces 10 inches square. Grease each leaf and place ¼ cup grated apio, spread it out into a rectangular shape about 9″ x 5″. Put about ¼ cup filling along one side. Fold the leaf lengthwise so edges of mixture meet, turn sides toward middle and fold under. Bake in a moderate oven 350°F for 45 minutes.

EMPANADA DE YUCA

EMPANADA DE PLATANO

EMPANADA DE YAUTIA

Follow directions for Empanada de Apio.

PASTELÓN DE APIO
Apio Pie

6 servings

4 cups grated apio
3 tablespoons achote coloring

Salt to taste
2 cups meat filling

Season the apio and add the achote coloring. Arrange half of the mixture in a greased pie-tin and cover bottom and sides as for pie. Put in the meat filling. Cover surface with the rest of the apio mixture. Bake in a moderate oven 350°F for 45 minutes.

POTATO PIE
Pastelón de Papa   6 servings

2 pounds potatoes	4 tablespoons flour
1 teaspoon salt	2 cups meat filling
2 beaten eggs	

Boil and mash the potatoes. Add the salt, eggs and flour. Divide
mixture into two parts. Put one part in a greased pie-tin and spread
out to cover bottom and sides. Put in the meat filling and spread
over bottom. Cover with the rest of the potato mixture. Bake in a
moderate oven at 350°F for 30 to 40 minutes.

PASTELÓN DE PLÁTANO

PASTELÓN DE YAUTÍA BLANCA

Follow directions for Pastelón de Apio.

SALADS

LETTUCE SALAD   6 servings

1 bunch lettuce	2 tablespoons vinegar
1 clove garlic	2 tablespoons olive oil
1 sliced onion	½ teaspoon salt
1 ripe pepper	

Clean and wash lettuce leaves carefully. Peel garlic and rub sides
and bottom of salad bowl, to have garlic flavor. Place lettuce leaves.
Mix vinegar, oil and salt. Pour over lettuce leaves. Garnish with
slices of onion and ripe pepper.

WATERCRESS SALAD   6 servings

Use watercress instead of lettuce and garnish with olives and strips
of pimento.

CUCUMBER SALAD   6 servings

3 cucumbers	2 tablespoons vinegar
½ teaspoon salt	2 tablespoons olive oil

Remove stems from cucumbers. Slice crosswise. Mix vinegar, oil, and
salt. Arrange salad and pour over dressing. Garnish with sliced olives.

BAKED PEPPER SALAD   8 servings

10 green peppers   1 teaspoon salt
½ cup olive oil   ¼ teaspoon pepper
¼ cup vinegar

Bake peppers. Place in cold water, remove skin and seeds and cut
into strips. Mix vinegar, oil, salt and pepper. Arrange pepper in bowl
and pour over dressing.

STRING BEAN SALAD   6 servings

1 pound boiled string beans   ¼ cup vinegar
1 sliced onion   1 teaspoon salt
2 sliced tomatoes   ¼ teaspoon pepper
¼ cup olive oil   1 ground clove garlic

Mix oil, vinegar, salt, pepper and garlic and let stand. Arrange string
beans in salad bowl. Strain dressing and pour over salad. Garnish
with tomatoes and onion.

LETTUCE AND TOMATO SALAD   8 servings

1 bunch lettuce   2 tablespoon vinegar
1 pound tomatoes   ½ teaspoon salt
4 tablespoons olive oil

Wash lettuce carefully, drain, and arrange in salad bowl. Slice tomatoes and place on leaves. Mix oil, vinegar, and salt and pour over
salad.

CHAYOTE SALAD   6 servings

3 chayotes   4 tablespoons olive oil
2 ripe peppers   2 tablespoons vinegar
1 bunch lettuce   ½ teaspoon salt

Wash chayotes, cut in halves and boil. Bake red peppers, remove
seeds, wash and cut into strips. Wash lettuce leaves. Mix oil, vinegar
and salt. When chayotes are cooked, cool, remove skin and cut in
cubes. Place cubes in bowl, and add one half of the dressing, stir
well. Arrange chayotes on lettuce leaves, garnish with strips of red
pepper and pour over dressing.

EGGS AND POTATO SALAD

6 servings

6 hard boiled eggs	4 tablespoons olive oil
6 boiled potatoes	2 tablespoons vinegar
1 sliced small onion	1 teaspoon salt
1 sliced green pepper	1 bunch lettuce

Wash lettuce and arrange in salad bowl. Slice eggs and potatoes. Arrange on lettuce alternating one slice of potato and a slice of egg. Garnish with onion and pepper. Pour over dressing.

PICKLED NAVY BEANS

8 servings

1 pound navy beans	$\frac{1}{4}$ cup vinegar
$\frac{1}{2}$ cup olive oil	8 peppercorns
2 sliced onions	1 bay leaf
3 cloves garlic	1 tablespoon salt

Wash and cook beans. Drain and cool. Heat oil, add onion and peeled garlic and fry slightly to wilt onion. Add vinegar and other ingredients. Place beans in bowl and pour over dressing.

For other vegetable recipes please see Chapters V and VI.

CHAPTER VIII

CEREALS AND THE LEGUMES

Rice is one of the earliest food plants introduced in Puerto Rico. It was brought by Columbus in his second trip to America in 1493, when he discovered this island.

Rice and beans, the most typical food combination, is considered the basic diet of Puerto Rico, and is the main dish of families with low income levels. Rice is also served with legumes or combined with pork, fish, poultry and vegetables. "Arroz con pollo" is a very popular dish as well as the "asopao", a more recent invention.

BOILED RICE   **6 servings**
Arroz Blanco

1 pound rice	2 cups water
2 tablespoons fat	2 teaspoons salt

Wash rice. Heat fat in an iron kettle (caldero), add rice and mix well. Add salted water, stir and allow to boil. As soon as the water has been absorbed, reduce the heat and cover. Stir two or three times and cook until the rice grain is cooked. Serve hot. See illustration.

STEWED RICE AND BEANS   **8 servings**
Arroz con Habichuelas

1 tablespoon chopped salt pork	2 teaspoons salt
2 ounces chopped smoked ham	1 pound rice
1 chopped green pepper	1 pound cooked beans
1 chopped tomato	2 cups water
1 chopped onion	Achote coloring as desired
2 ground cloves garlic	

Sauté salt pork and ham in an iron kettle, add green peppers, tomato, onion and garlic and cook over low heat a few minutes. Add rice and vegetables and mix well, then add beans, salt and water. Cook slowly until all the water has been absorbed, then cover until the rice is tender. Add achote coloring as desired. Serve hot.

[86]

HOW TO EXTRACT COCOANUT MILK

Break dry cocoanut to remove water. Cut shell into several large pieces. Place in oven and heat to remove shell easily. Break nut into pieces, remove the brown skin and grate. To a dry grated cocoanut add about 1 or 2 cups hot water. Strain through a fine cloth or sieve. Do not add any water, if more concentrated milk is desired.

COWPEAS AND RICE WITH COCOANUT MILK   8 servings

2 ounces chopped smoked ham
2 ounces chopped salt pork
1 chopped sweet pepper
1 sprig parsley
2 teaspoons salt

1 ground clove garlic
2 chopped tomatoes
2½ cups cocoanut milk
1 pound cowpeas

Sauté ham and salt pork. Add green pepper, garlic, tomato, parsley and ½ cup cocoanut milk and simmer for a few minutes. Add rice and stir, add peas, salt and remaining cocoanut milk. Let come to a boil, lower the heat and when almost dry cover and cook until the rice is tender. Serve hot.

STEWED RICE AND PIGEON PEAS   8 servings
Arroz con Gandules

1 tablespoon chopped salt pork
2 ounces chopped smoked ham[1]
2 chopped green peppers
2 chopped tomatoes
1 chopped onion
2 ground cloves garlic
2 chopped sweet peppers

1 tablespoon capers
2 tablespoons olives
1 teaspoon salt
1 tablespoon achote coloring
1 pound boiled fresh pigeon peas
1 pound rice
2 cups water[2]

Sauté ham and salt pork. Add peppers, tomatoes, onion and garlic and simmer for a few minutes. Add capers, olives, achote coloring and pigeon peas. Mix well and let cook for two or three minutes. Add water, salt and rice. Mix thoroughly. Cook slowly until the liquid has evaporated. Stir, cover and cook until the rice is tender. Serve hot.

---

[1] Fresh pork spare ribs may be added too. Boil them with the pigeon peas.
[2] Use the water in which the pigeon peas were boiled.

[87]

RICE, GARDEN STYLE — 6 servings

1 diced onion
1 diced ripe pepper
¼ cut olive oil
1 chopped clove garlic
2 diced tomatoes
½ pound string beans, cut into 1" pieces

1 diced carrot
½ pound pumpkin cut into ½" cubes
1 tablespoon achote coloring
1 pound rice
2 teaspoon salt
2 cups water or broth

Sauté onion and pepper in olive oil. Add garlic, tomato, string beans, carrots and pumpkin. Stir and simmer for fifteen minutes. Add achote coloring, rice, salt and liquid. Cook slowly until the liquid has evaporated. Cover and stir once or twice until the rice is tender. Serve hot.

RICE AND VEGETABLES — 6 to 8 servings

1 ounce chopped salt pork
2 ounces chopped smoked ham
2 diced tomatoes
1 diced green pepper
1 diced onion
1 ground garlic
1 sprig parsley
1 pound rice

½ pound cooked chick-peas
½ pound string beans cut into 1" pieces
2 teaspoons salt
3 ripe peppers cut into 1" pieces
2 cups water
2 cups cabbage, cut into 1" pieces.

Fry the salt pork then add ham, tomatoes, green pepper, onion, garlic, parsley and simmer for a few minutes. Add rice, mix well then add chick-peas, string beans, salt and water. Cook over low heat until liquid has been absorbed. Add cabbage and ripe peppers and cover with a piece of plantain leaf. Stir once or twice. Serve hot.

RICE AND OKRA — 6 servings

3 tablespoons olive oil
½ pound okra cut into ½" pieces
1 chopped onion
¼ cup tomato sauce

1 teaspoon vinegar
2 cups rice
2 cups water
2 teaspoons salt

Sauté onion, add okra and stir to mix well. Add tomato sauce, vinegar and simmer for about ten minutes. Add rice, stir then add liquid and salt, mix and cook over low heat, until all the liquid has been absorbed, then cover and continue cooking till the rice is tender. Serve hot.

[88]

RICE AND PORK MEAT   6 to 8 servings
Arroz con Carne de Cerdo

1 pound pork meat cut into small pieces	2 teaspoon salt
1 ounce diced salt pork	2 diced tomatoes
2 ounces diced smoked ham	1 pound rice
1 ground clove garlic	1 tablespoon achote coloring
1 diced green pepper	2 cups water

Sauté meat, salt pork, ham, tomato, green pepper, garlic and simmer until the meat is tender. Add rice and mix well, then add achote coloring, water and salt. Cook slowly until all the water has been absorbed, then cover till the rice is tender, stir only once or twice while cooking. Serve hot.

RICE AND LINK SAUSAGES   6 servings

2 tablespoons fat	6 link sausages cut into ½" pieces
2 ounces chopped smoked ham	1 pound rice
1 chopped onion	1 tablespoon achote coloring
1 chopped tomato	2 cups water
1 chopped green pepper	2 teaspoons salt

Sauté ham, add tomato, onion pepper and sausages. Mix well, add rice and cook for two minutes, add achote coloring, salt and water, mix thoroughly and cook over low heat until all the water has been absorbed, then cover until rice is tender. Serve hot.

NOTE: Spanish sausage, longaniza, or any other kind may be used.

CHICKEN AND RICE   6 to 8 servings
Arroz con Pollo

1—2½ pounds ready to cook chicken, cut up	1 tablespoon capers
2 chopped cloves garlic	¼ cup olives
½ teaspoon ground orégano	1 pound rice
2 teaspoons salt	1 tablespoon achote coloring
2 chopped tomatoes	2 cups water or broth
1 chopped green pepper	4 pimentos
1 chopped onion	1 cup peas

Mix salt, garlic and orégano and rub chicken inside and out. Sauté tomatoes, pepper and onion. Add chicken and simmer half an hour. Add achote coloring, rice, olives and capers, mix well. Add liquid, stir and cook until all the water has been absorbed then cover until the rice is done. Serve hot. Garnish with strips of pimentos and peas.

CHICKEN ASOPAO

6 to 8 servings

1—2½ pounds ready to cook chicken	2 cups rice
2 tablespoons lard	2 teaspoons salt
2 ounces chopped smoked ham	6 cups water
1 chopped onion	1 tablespoon capers
1 chopped green pepper	¼ cup olives
2 chopped tomatoes	1 cup peas
1 ground clove garlic	4 pimentos
	½ cup Parmesan cheese

Cut chicken in small serving pieces, rub each piece with salt, orégano and garlic. Brown it in lard, then add ham, onion, tomato and pepper. Cover and simmer for half an hour. Remove bones from chicken and put it again in the pot, add water, capers and olives and cook for five minutes, then add rice, season to taste and simmer until the rice is tender and still moist ("asopao"). Garnish with peas, strips of pimento and grated cheese. The asopao must be served immediately as soon as removed from heat otherwise it will dry out.

RICE, PAELLA STYLE
Arroz a la Paella

8 servings

1—2 pound ready to cook chicken cut up	3 cups broth
1 pound pork meat, cut into 1″ pieces	¼ cup olive oil
	2 chopped onions
½ pound fish, cut into 1″ pieces	2 chopped tomatoes
	2 chopped green peppers
3 teaspoons salt	1 cup shrimps
1 teaspoon ground orégano	8 clams
8 artichoke hearts	3 cups rice

Rub chicken, pork meat and fish with salt and orégano. Prepare a broth using the wings, neck and bones from the meat. Heat olive oil and sauté the onion, tomato the pepper. Add chicken, pork and fish, mix well and simmer for thirty minutes. Add shrimps, clams and broth. Cover and cook for five minutes. Add rice and season to taste. Cook over low heat and when almost done add artichokes and peas. If possible serve in the same pot it was cooked. Garnish with strips of pimento.

RICE AND FISH 6 to 8 servings

1½ pounds whole fish
2 teaspoons salt
½ cup olive oil or fat
3½ cups water
1 onion
1 clove garlic
1 tablespoon salt

3 cups fish broth
1 diced onion
2 diced peppers
3 diced tomatoes
1 chopped clove garlic
½ cup olive oil
1½ pounds rice

Cut fish in pieces, rub with salt and fry in fat or oil. Boil together head and tail of fish, onion and garlic. Strain and measure 3 cups broth. Fry slightly onion, pepper, tomatoes and garlic in olive oil. Add rice and stir, cook for few minutes. Add the fish broth and let cook until rice is almost done. Cut fish in small pieces and add to rice, stir to mix well. Lower the heat, cover and cook until rice is tender. Stir once or twice before removing from heat.

RICE AND SHRIMPS

Follow directions for Rice and Fish, using shrimps instead of fish, and water instead of broth.

RICE WITH FISH AND VEGETABLES 8–10 servings

5 ripe peppers
4 tablespoons olive oil
3 cloves garlic
2 cups green beans[3]
1 cup string beans cut into 1″ pieces

3 tomatoes
1 tablespoon salt
3 cups water
1½ pounds rice
2 tablespoons achote coloring
1½ pounds fried fish

Clean peppers, fry slightly, remove from oil and cut into small pieces. Fry slightly the green and string beans, tomato and garlic. Add water, salt and boil for 10 minutes; then add rice and achote coloring. When most of the water has evaporated add fish cut into small pieces and

---

[3] Green beans is the mature bean, but removed from the pod before it dries, it is sold at the market by the pound.

[91]

peppers, stir. Lower the heat, cover and let cook until rice is tender. It may be stirred once or twice.

RICE AND CODFISH   6–8 servings
Arroz con Bacalao

½ pound salt codfish	½ cup olive oil
2 ounces salt pork	⅓ cup olives
1 chopped onion	1 tablespoon capers
2 chopped ripe peppers	3 cups water
3 chopped tomatoes	1½ pounds rice
1 ground clove garlic	Salt to taste and coloring

Soak codfish in water for several hours to remove most of the salt, remove skin and bones and cut into small pieces. Fry vegetables slightly in olive oil, add garlic, capers and olives; stir and cook for 1 minute. Add water, salt to taste and boil, then add rice and vegetable coloring. Cook until almost dry. Lower the heat, stir and cover. Stir once or twice and remove from heat when rice grain is tender.

CORNMEAL

Cornmeal is one of the oldest crops grown in Puerto Rico since colonial times. Cornmeal is used for such popular dishes as "funche" and "surullitos". It is also combined with other foods: meat, fish and cocoanut to prepare several dishes such as ' hayacas" and "funche con coco".

FUNCHE   6 servings

4 cups water	1 teaspoon salt
1 cup cornmeal	1 tablespoon pork fat

Mix cornmeal and salt. Add water slowly and stir to prevent lumps. Cook at low heat stirring constantly until mixture gets thick and cornmeal is tender. Add fat, stir and remove from heat. Milk may be used instead of water; it may be cooked in a double boiler.

FUNCHE AND COCOANUT MILK   6–8 servings

1 dry cocoanut	1 teaspoon salt
1 cup cornmeal	¾ cup sugar
1 stick cinnamon	Ground cinnamon

Extract the cocoanut milk and add enough water to get 4 cups. Mix

[92]

all ingredients and cook for 20 minutes at low heat, stirring constantly. Remove from heat when cornmeal is tender and dry. Serve and sprinkle on top with cinnamon.

FUNCHE AND FISH
6 to 8 servings

1 pound fish	1 teaspoon salt
6 cups water	1 cup cornmeal

Boil fish, remove bones and mince. Use 4 cups of water in which fish was boiled, add cornmeal and cook slowly, stirring constantly. When most of the water has evaporated add the minced fish, stir. Add salt to taste, cook until dry and serve. Salted codfish may be used instead of fish.

GUANIMES
10 guanimes

1 pound cornmeal	1 cup cocoanut milk
1 teaspoon salt	½ teaspoon anise seeds
2 tablespoons sugar	¼ cup water

Mix cornmeal, salt and sugar. Boil anise seeds in water, strain and add to cocoanut milk. Add milk to cornmeal to get a dough. Divide in 10 equal parts. Roll each part on a greased 8″ square of plantain leaf. Roll and tie ends. Boil in salted water for 30 minutes.

NOTE: Guanimes may also be made from grated green plantain.

HAYACAS
18 hayacas

1 pound pearl hominy	½ cup achote coloring
3 quarts water	2 tablespoons salt

Clean pearl hominy to remove yellow grains, and wash. Place in water the night before or for 10 hours. Boil until hominy is tender; while cooking stir occassionally to prevent sticking to bottom of kettle. Remove from heat, strain and wash hominy several times to remove some of the loose starch. Grind with finest knife. Add salt to taste, achote coloring and mix well so mixture can be spread easily. Keep covered in refrigerator until ready to use.

Filling

1 pound pork meat	½ cup raisins
3 ounces smoked ham	3 ounces shelled almonds
1 onion	4 sliced hard boiled eggs
1 green pepper	3 sliced onions
2 tomatoes	3 pimentos cut into strips
2 tablespoons fat	Achote coloring
2 teaspoons salt	4 packages plantain leaves
1 cup olives	
2 tablespoons halved capers	

Grind meat, ham, onion, pepper and tomatoes in food chopper, add salt and cook for 5 minutes. Remove from heat and add olives, capers and raisins. Wash and trim plantain leaves, cut into 10″ squares. Spread achote coloring over leaf and take 2 tablespoonfuls of dough and extend on leaf, in rectangular shape. Put one tablespoon meat filling along center, and place on top a slice of egg, onion, a strip of pimento and an almond. Fold over dough, so edges will meet, fold again to a rectangular shape about 3½″ wide and 7″ long. Fold ends of plantain leaf under. Put hayacas in pairs, with folded ends inside and tie. Cook for 30 minutes in boiling salted water. Remove from water and let drain few minutes before serving, so they will hold the shape.

MACARONI PRODUCTS

We have incorporated into our cookery some of the Italian recipes but have developed a dish entirely different from its original form. To the macaroni products we add pork, chicken or sausage. To the dough for the ravioli an egg is added.

SPAGHETTI SAUCE

1 chopped onion	1 bay leaf
¼ cup olive oil	1 teaspoon sugar
4 cloves chopped garlic	1 teaspoon salt
1 cup tomato sauce	½ teaspoon peppercorns
1 No. 2½ can tomatoes	

Sauté the onion in the olive oil. Add the other ingredients and cook over low heat until sauce thickens which will require about half an hour. Mash and strain.

MACARONI AND MAJORCA SAUSAGE
8–10 servings

1 pound boiled elbow macaroni
¼ pound chopped smoked
ham
½ cup olive oil
2 sliced onions

¼ pound minced Majorca sausage
1 chopped clove garlic
1 cup tomato paste
1 cup water
2 teaspoons salt

Sauté the ham, in the olive oil and add the onions, garlic, sausage, tomato paste, water and salt to taste. Cover and cook at low heat for 15 minutes. Add the macaroni, stir and cook for few minutes. Remove from heat.

MACARONI AND PORK
8–10 servings

Follow directions for Macaroni and Majorca Sausage. Use one pound of pork cut into 1½ inch cubes instead of Majorca sausage. Cook until pork is tender and then add the macaroni. Add ½ cup grated Parmesan cheese before serving.

SPAGHETTI AND CHICKEN
8–10 servings

1—3 pounds ready to cook
stewing chicken cut up
¼ pound sliced onions
1 bay leaf
1 chopped clove garlic
¼ teaspoon pepper
1 pound boiled spaghetti

2 chopped ripe peppers
½ cup olive oil
1 cup tomato sauce
1 tablespoon salt
1 tablespoon vinegar
½ cup grated Parmesan cheese

Sauté the onions, garlic and ripe peppers in olive oil. Add bay leaf, pepper, tomato sauce, salt and vinegar, mix well. Add chicken and cover dish, cook at low heat, for 30 minutes. When chicken is tender, remove flesh from bones. Cut spaghetti into 3″ strips and mix with chicken stew. Cook at a low heat for few minutes. Before serving add half the cheese and stir. Serve in a dish with rest of cheese sprinkled on top.

CANELONES 6 servings

½ pound canelones
2 quarts water
1 tablespoon olive oil or lard
1 pound ground pork meat
¼ pound ground ham
2 teaspoons salt

½ teaspoon pepper
2 chopped onions
1 teaspoon salt
2 tablespoons fat
½ cup grated Parmesan cheese
3 cups spaghetti sauce

Boil the canelones with the olive oil and the salt. When they are partly done, remove from the water and arrange each canelon separately on a plate, to avoid sticking together. Mix the pork meat, ham, onion, pepper, salt and fat and cook over low heat. Add 2 tablespoons of cheese to the meat and stir well. Stuff the canelones. Into a greased baking dish put a layer of canelones and pour over half the spaghetti sauce and cheese. Repeat. Bake in a moderate oven for 20 minutes.

RAVIOLI 8 servings

3 cups flour
1 egg
Warm water
1 pound chicken meat or pork
    meat
½ brain
1 tablespoon salt
2 onions

6 cups water
1 chopped onion
1 chopped tablespoon parsley
½ teaspoon pepper
½ cup grated Parmesan cheese
2 eggs
3 cups spaghetti sauce

To make the dough, put the flour into a bowl, make a little well in the center of the flour and put in the egg (yolks and whites). Stir until well blended, and add the warm water little by little to form a soft dough that does not stick to the hands. Knead the dough a bit and set it aside for one hour. To begin the filling, heat the water. Add the salt, onion, meat and the brain and boil for 15 minutes. Grind the meat, brain, onion, and parsley in the grinder, using the finest cutter. Season and sauté for ten minutes, then add the eggs and the grated cheese, stir and remove from heat. Take a portion of the dough and roll it out thin with the rolling pin. Cut the dough in a rectangular square about 2½″ x 4½″ to form the ravioli. Put a half teaspoonful of filling on the cut-out dough; bring moistened edges together and prick edges firmly with a fork to join them. Cook the ravioli in the water in which the meat and brain were boiled over low heat for 25 minutes or until they are cooked. Remove from the water and put the ravioli in a greased baking-dish. Pour the spaghetti sauce over them, and sprinkle top with grated Parmesan cheese. Put the dish into a moderate oven for 20 minutes.

NOTE: The ravioli may also be cooked in an earthenware dish or in a kettle, over low heat; instead of in the oven.

LEGUMES (BEANS)

Legumes are a cheap source of protein and also contain vitamins and iron salts. The protein of the legumes is incomplete[4] except in the soy bean, chick peas and pigeon peas. Red or kidney beans is the most popular of the legumes consumed here, but is not produced in large quantities and is difficult to get in the market. The protein of chick peas (garbanzos) and pigeon peas is of excellent quality and is a good source of calcium. Pigeon peas (gandules) is one of the most popular legumes consumed here and is marketed and eaten both fresh or "green" and dry. Chick peas was the main item of food in the "rancho" served to the Spanish soldier during colonial days; and they were called "the conquerors of America" by one of our historians.

Most common legumes found at the market are:

Chick-peas	garbanzos
Cow-peas	frijoles
Kidney beans	habichuelas coloradas
Lentils	lentejas
Lima beans	habas
Navy beans	habichuelas blancas
Pigeon peas	gandules

General directions for cooking legumes

Pick legumes to remove any foreign particle or imperfect grains. Wash and soak in water for four hours to replace the water evaporated. The length of soaking time has no effect upon cooking time. Water should be soft; hard water seems to retard cooking time. Never add bicarbonate of soda to the soaking water because it destroys the thiamin present in legumes. If dried lima beans are to be cooked in a pressure cooker, they retain their shape better and have a better texture if cooked without soaking, but the cooking period is longer.

---

[4] They do not contain all the amino acids.

[97]

FRESH LEGUMES

FRESH NAVY BEAN STEW   10 servings

1½ pounds beans   ½ cup sofrito
½ pound pumpkin cut into   Salt to taste
  pieces

Parboil the beans. Add the sofrito and the pumpkin. Cook over low
heat until beans are tender and broth thickens. Season to taste and
remove from heat.

NOTE: Fresh pigeon peas are prepared in the same way.

PIGEON PEAS WITH PLANTAIN   10 servings
BALLS

1 pound fresh pigeon peas   1 cup pumpkin cut into small
1 cilantro leaf   cubes
1 sweet pepper   1 green plantain grated
4 cups water   Salt to taste
½ cup sofrito

Boil the pigeon peas with the cilantro and sweet pepper until the
peas are soft, add the sofrito. Season the grated plantain to taste
and form it into small balls. Add the balls to the peas with the pumpkin. Allow to cook at low heat until the plantain balls are done and
the sauce is thick.

DRY LEGUMES

RED BEAN STEW   10 servings

1 pound red beans soaked   ½ cup sofrito
½ pound pumpkin cut into 1 Salt to taste
  inch cubes

Cook the beans and when they begin to boil lower the heat and cook
until they are quite soft. Add the sofrito and the pumpkin. Season
and continue cooking over low heat. Remove from heat when the
sauce is thick and the beans thoroughly done. See illustration.

NOTE: Chick peas, lentils, and black-eyed pea stew are made in
    the same way.

KIDNEY BEAN STEW WITH
RIPE PLANTAIN
10 servings

1 pound beans, soaked	1 tablespoon sugar
½ cup sofrito	2 tablespoons butter
1 ripe plantain, sliced	1 stick cinnamon
Salt to taste	

Boil the beans until somewhat tender, about an hour. Add the sofrito, plantain and other ingredients. Cook at low heat until the plantain is done and the sauce is thick. Season to taste and remove from heat.

FRIED CHICK PEAS
10 servings

1 pound cooked chick peas	Olive oil or fat
Salt to taste	

Skin the chick peas, add a little salt, fry over low heat until golden brown.

CHAPTER IX

BEVERAGES

Cold drinks are a necessity in a tropical country. In Puerto Rico there is an abundance of citrus fruits: oranges, lemons, limes, grape-fruits, sour oranges and pineapple for preparing appetizing cold drinks and desserts. In addition the pulp of the soursop, guava, tamarind and West Indian cherry are delicious in cold drinks and "horchatas". The pineapple peelings are used for a cold drink known as "garapiña".

Besides quenching the thirst, fruit drinks are a valuable source of vitamins and mineral salts. In order to preserve the fruit flavor, use enough sugar to give a sweet taste. A teaspoon of lemon juice added to cold drinks prepared with soursop, papaya or guava will accent the fruit flavor.

The most popular hot beverage is coffee. The Puerto Rican style of serving coffee is a cup of hot milk with one or two teaspoonfuls of coffee extract; this is known as "café con leche". To prepare this coffee extract a finely ground coffee is used, and it is drip or filtered. This is a very strong coffee which must be diluted to suit your taste when served as after dinner coffee.

Coffee flavor is very delicate; it is affected by oxygen in the air. While it is being dripped as much air as possible, should be excluded. To preserve the good flavor of coffee and prevent the extract from getting rancid, place it in a glass bottle with a tight stopper and keep in the refrigerator.

Hot chocolate is another favorite beverage. Spanish style, is served with milk, sugar and vanilla. Chocolate is considered a luxury drink, it was the traditional hot beverage served at our grandmothers' weddings, and for that occasion was made richer by adding egg yolks and butter. When friends greeted the bride-to-be and inquired about her wedding, they used to say, "When are you offering us hot choco-late?"

COLD DRINKS

WEST INDIAN CHERRY DRINK
Refresco de Cereza

6–8 servings

3 cups cherries   ½ cup sugar
6 cups water

Mash the cherries adding sugar slowly. Add water, stir well and strain. If necessary add more sugar. Serve cold. Garnish with orange slices.

GUAVA DRINK

6–8 servings

1 pound ripe guavas   4 cups cold water
1 cup sugar

Cut guavas in quarters and remove seeds. Mash pulp and strain. Add sugar and water. Serve cold and garnish with lemon slices.

PAPAYA DRINK

6–8 servings

2 cups ripe papaya pulp   4 cups water
1 cup sugar

Mix pulp and sugar. Add water slowly and strain. Serve cold and garnish with native cherry.

PINEAPPLE DRINK

6–8 servings

2 cups water   1 cup sugar
4 cups pineapple juice

Boil water and sugar for few minutes and let cool. Add pineapple juice. Serve cold garnished with native cherries or orange slices.

GARAPIÑA

Place pineapple peelings in a pitcher or a wide-mouth jar. Add water. Cover and let stand for twenty four hours until it ferments. Strain, add sugar to taste and serve very cold.

LEMONADE   6–8 servings
Limonada

1 cup sugar   6 cups water
Juice of 6 lemons

Mix sugar and water and heat to dissolve the sugar. Cool. Add lemon
juice and serve cold. Garnish with native cherry.

TAMARIND DRINK   8–10 servings
Refresco de Tamarindo

½ pound tamarind pods   6 cups water
1½ cups sugar

Remove seeds from pod. Mash pulp and discard seeds. Add sugar to
pulp and mix well. Add water and strain. Serve cold.

MOLARIND   6–8 servings
Melarindo

3 cups tamarind pulp   1½ cups molasses
6 cups water

Remove seeds from pulp. Add molasses and mash. Add water, mix
well and strain. Serve cold, garnish with lemon leaves.

GENIPAP DRINK   6 servings
Refresco de Jagua

4 genipap   4 cups water
1 cup sugar

Wash fruits, cut in pieces and grind. Add water and let stand for 30
minutes. Strain and add sugar. Serve cold.

COCOANUT DRINK   6–8 servings

2 cups grated dry cocoanut   4 cups cold water
2 cups hot water   ¾ cups sugar
Peel of 1 lemon

Add hot water to cocoanut. Place in cheese cloth and squeeze out the
"milk". Add cold water, lemon peeling and sugar to cocoanut "milk".
Serve cold and garnish with native red cherries.

SESAME SEEDS DRINK
6–8 servings
Horchata de Ajonjolí

2 cups sesame seeds	4 cups hot water
2 cups cold water	1 cup sugar

Wash seeds and place in water for two hours. Grind in a mortar or meat chopper using finest grinder. Add hot water and squeeze out "milk" in a cheese cloth. Add sugar and cold water. Serve very cold and garnish with mint leaves or lemon slices.

SOURSOP DRINK
6–8 servings
Refresco de Guanábana

4 cups water	3 cups soursop pulp
1½ cups sugar	2 teaspoons lemon juice

Mash soursop pulp with sugar, add water and strain. Add lemon juice and serve cold. Garnish with native cherry.

SOURSOP MILK DRINK
6–8 servings
Champola de Guanábana

1 ripe soursop	1½ cups sugar
Water	4 cups cold milk

Add enough water to soursop to get 3 cups juice or nectar. Place in refrigerator to cool. Mix sugar and milk and add cold juice slowly. Serve cold and garnish with orange slices.

WINE AND LEMON DRINK
6 servings
Sangría

3 cups water	1½ cups red Spanish wine
½ cup sugar	2 tablespoons lemon juice

Mix water and sugar and heat to dissolve sugar. Let cool. Add wine and lemon juice. Serve very cold.

BEER AND LEMON JUICE DRINK
4–6 servings
Bul

1 bottle beer	4 tablespoons lemon juice
2 bottles soda water	Sugar

Mix ingredients at the time of serving. Add lemon juice and sugar to taste. Serve cold.

[103]

AGUALOJA

6-8 servings

1 pound ginger root
½ ounce cinnamon bark

5 cups water
1½ cups molasses

Mince ginger, add water and cinnamon and boil. Strain and let cool. Add molasses and serve cold.

MABÍ

6 servings

2½ cups water
1 ounce mabí bark
2 cups lukewarm water

¾ cups brown sugar
1¼ cups mabí[1]

Boil mabí bark in 2½ cups water until it takes a golden color. Strain and stir until tea becomes foamy. Add lukewarm water, sugar and mabí. Stir again. Place in bottles and let ferment for 24 hours.

TROPICAL PUNCH

8-10 servings

2 cups water
2 cups sugar
2 cups pineapple juice

2 cups grapefruit juice
2 cups orange juice

Heat water and sugar until the sugar is dissolved. Let cool. Add the fruit juices. Serve cold. Garnish with lemon and orange slices.

LEMON AND BEER PUNCH

6-8 servings

1 cup water
1 cup sugar
1 cup lemon juice

½ cup grapefruit juice
1 bottle beer

Heat the water and dissolve sugar. Cool. Add the fruit juices and water. Add beer just before serving. This is the rule whenever carbonated drinks such as beer are added. Place block of ice in punch bowl and pour punch over it.

MINT JULEP

20 servings

½ cup lemon juice
1 cup sugar
1 bunch fresh mint leaves

½ cup water
2 quarts ginger ale
Ice

Mix lemon juice, sugar and water. Add mint leaves. Allow to stand for 30 minutes. Add ice and ginger ale just before serving.

[1] The drink already prepared to aid fermentation.

FRUIT PUNCH

20–25 punch cups

4 cups water
2½ cups sugar
2 cups orange juice
1 cup lemon juice

¾ cup pineapple juice
1 cup crushed pineapple
1½ cups diced bananas
1 cup native cherries

Heat water to dissolve sugar. Cool. Add fruit juices and water. Add fruits before serving. Pour over block of ice in punch bowl.

ORANGE PUNCH

5–6 servings

6 egg yolks
1 cup sugar
4 cups orange juice

2 egg whites
4 tablespoons sugar

Beat yolks and add sugar. Add orange juice, mix well and strain. Serve very cold and garnish with beaten whites.

HOT BEVERAGES

COFFEE EXTRACT
Café

8–10 servings

1 cup ground coffee   1¼ cups boiling water

Place coffee in coffee drip. Add boiling water, ¼ cup at a time. Let drip slowly until all water is added. Place in glass bottle and keep in refrigerator.

AFTER DINNER COFFEE
Café Negro

To 1 cup coffee extract add about 1½ to 3 cups boiling water and serve as "café negro" or after dinner coffee.

HOT CHOCOLATE

8 servings

4 ounces sweet chocolate[2]   6 cups milk

Grate chocolate. Heat milk, when milk boils add chocolate and beat for few minutes. Let boil again and beat again for three times, so it is foamy.

---

[2] If bitter chocolate is used add sugar to taste and a few drops vanilla for flavor.

WEDDING CHOCOLATE
12 to 15 servings
Chocolate de Boda

½ pound grated sweet chocolate
8 cups hot milk
1 can 14 ounces evaporated
milk (undiluted)

2 beaten egg yolks
4 tablespoons butter
¼ cup sugar

Add milk to chocolate and boil for few minutes. Add evaporated milk and sugar and continue cooking in a double boiler. Two minutes before serving add egg yolks and butter. Beat for two minutes and serve.

GINGER TEA
4 servings
Te de Jengibre

1—2" piece ginger root
4 cups water

8 teaspoons sugar

Wash ginger root and pound to flatten it. Add water and heat. When tea starts boiling cover and remove from heat. Strain, add sugar. Serve hot.

ORANGE LEAF TEA
4 servings

8 orange leaves
4 cups water

6 teaspoons sugar

Select tenderest orange leaves from bud. Cut up and place in water. When water boils, cover and remove from heat. Let stand three minutes. Strain and add sugar to taste. Serve hot.
    NOTE: This may be served with equal parts milk.

QUEEN'S EGGNOG
6 servings
Ponche de la Reina

2 cups hot milk
1 stick cinnamon
Peeling 1 lemon

4 egg yolks
¼ cup sugar
¼ teaspoon salt

Add cinnamon and lemon peeling to milk and boil. Beat egg yolk and add sugar and salt. Add milk slowly and stir well. Serve hot.

ALCOHOLIC DRINKS

ORANGE PUNCH
40 servings

7 cups orange juice

2½ cups Puerto Rican rum

2½ cups syrup

5 cups soda water

Mix ingredients in order given. Pour in punch bowl, add ice and garnish with slices of oranges, lemons and whole cherries.

RUM PUNCH
20 servings

2 cups Puerto Rican rum

20 crushed cherries

1 cup pineapple juice

½ cup sugar

4 cups soda water

Crushed ice

Mix rum, cherries, fruit juice and sugar. When ready to serve add soda water and crushed ice. Garnish with lemon slices and bits of pineapple.

C FIZZ
30 servings

4 egg yolks

¾ cup grenadine syrup

1 cup brandy

1 cup Claret wine

1 cup Vermouth

½ cup lemon juice

Beat yolks and add syrup. Add other ingredients and serve very cold.

RUM EGGNOG
15–20 servings

¼ cup sugar

2 cups Puerto Rican rum

4 eggs

4 cups milk

Cracked ice

Nutmeg

Put ingredients in cocktail shaker and mix well. Add cracked ice and shake. Strain and serve very cold. Sprinkle nutmeg on top.

CHRISTMAS EGGNOG
10–12 servings

5 yolks

½ cup sugar

2 tablespoons creme de cacao

1⅔ cups undiluted evaporated milk

¾ cup Puerto Rican rum

Beat yolks, add sugar, creme de cacao, evaporated milk and rum. Mix well and strain. Place in bottles and keep in refrigerator. Sprinkle top with cinnamon and serve cold.

CHRISTMAS PUNCH 20-25 servings

6 egg yolks
2½ cups sugar
3½ cups undiluted evaporated milk

1 cup Puerto Rican rum
1 tablespoon vanilla

Beat yolks; add sugar slowly and continue beating until creamy. Add milk and cook over low heat. Remove from heat before it boils. Allow to cool. Add rum and vanilla. Serve very cold.

HOT RUM AND MILK PUNCH 15-20 servings

4 egg yolks
¼ cup sugar
4 cups hot milk

2 cups Puerto Rican rum
Pinch nutmeg

Beat the yolks, add the sugar and continue beating until mixture is smooth. Add milk, rum and nutmeg. Strain and serve hot. May sprinkle more nutmeg on top.

CHAPTER X

DESSERTS

Our grandmothers did not have the conveniences we enjoy today so baking was not done so extensively as it is practiced now. Dishes requiring the use of an oven were sent to the commercial bakeries or "panaderías" to be baked. Sometimes the clever housewife improvised some device for baking the pudding or "flan". She would place over the fire a large pan containing hot water. The pudding pan was placed into the pan and covered. In order to keep an even distribution of heat, live charcoal was placed on top of the lid and very good results were obtained.

In the early days of the Spanish colonization, flour was very scarce, expensive, and almost a luxury article. When a Spanish vessel arrived with flour and other food supplies, the governor distributed the flour among the garrison and the clergy, and whatever was left was sold to the colonizers. Thus, there was not much flour left for cake making, or even for bread.

But in spite of the difficulties some good old fashioned cakes have come down to us such as "ponqué" (pound cake), "sopa borracha" (literally drunken soup), and "brazo gitano" (literally gypsy's arm). Other baked foods are some lard cookies known as "mantecados" and "polvorones". ———

CAKES AND COOKIES

PONQUÉ   20 servings

1 pound butter	½ teaspoon nutmeg
1 pound sugar	10 beaten whites
10 beaten yolks	2 tablespoons brandy
1 pound flour	

Cream the butter, add sugar gradually and beat for about 30 minutes or until mixture has a creamy consistency. Add yolks and continue beating. Sift the flour three times, add to the butter mixture and then add the rum. Fold in the whites. Pour mixture into an angel food cake pan and bake in a moderate oven (350° F) for 1 hour.

SPICE CAKE
Hojaldre

10 servings

6 eggs	2 teaspoons cinnamon
1¼ cups sugar	1 teaspoon cloves
2 cups flour	½ cup sweet wine
2 teaspoons baking powder	½ cup melted lard

Beat whole eggs until foamy. Add sugar gradually and continue beating to dissolve sugar. Mix flour, baking powder, cinnamon and cloves and sift three times. Mix melted lard and wine and add flour to eggs alternating with wine. Pour in a buttered angel food cake pan. Bake in a moderate oven (350° F) for 30 minutes.

GYPSY'S ARM
Brazo Gitano

10 servings

4 egg whites	1 cup flour
½ cup sifted sugar	1½ teaspoons baking powder
4 egg yolks	Pinch salt
½ cup sifted sugar	¾ pound guava jelly
3 tablespoons water	

Beat whites until they will form peaks when beater is withdrawn. Add ½ cup sugar gradually. Beat egg yolks until thick and add another ½ cup sugar. Mix the whites and yolks and add water. Sift together flour, baking powder and salt and sift three times. Fold into the egg mixture. Line the bottom of a jelly roll pan with paper and grease paper. Pour the mixture and bake in a moderate oven (365° F) for 15 minutes. Take out from oven and turn out into a damp towel sprinkled with sugar. Remove paper and cut off strips on sides and ends if crusty. Beat jelly to cream consistency. Spread evenly on cake. Roll carefully, beginning with the long side, into a cylinder. Sprinkle with powdered sugar and place on a tray. For this recipe use a pan 16″ x 11″. If pan is larger increase ingredients in proportion.

TIPSY CAKE
Sopa Borracha

12 servings

6 beaten whites	1 cup flour
6 beaten yolks	Pinch salt
1 cup sugar	

Beat whites, add yolks and continue beating, add salt and sugar gradually. Fold in the flour. Pour mixture into an ungreased tube pan. Bake in a moderate oven (350° F) for 40 minutes.

SYRUP

2 cups sugar   1 cup sweet wine
½ cup water

Boil sugar and water. When syrup is thick remove from heat. Let cool and add wine. Stir well. Place cake in plate and pour over syrup.

TOPPING

2 egg whites   3 tablespoons comfits
2 tablespoons sugar

Beat egg whites until foamy, add sugar. Spread over cake and sprinkle comfits over.

BIENMESABE   10 servings
It Tastes Good to Me

1 large cocoanut   2 cups sugar
¼ cup hot water   ½ cup water
6 egg yolks   1 sponge cake

Grate the cocoanut. Add one fourth cup hot water and squeeze out the milk. Boil sugar and water until syrup threads from tines of fork. Mix cocoanut milk and beaten egg yolks. Add syrup to egg mixture slowly and cook in double boiler. Stir until it becomes slightly thick. Pour sauce over slices of sponge cake. See illustration.

MOCHA CAKE   8 servings
Torta Moca

¼ cup butter   1 sponge cake
1 cup sugar   2 ounces toasted almonds,
1 cup coffee extract   chopped
2 egg yolks

Cream butter, add sugar gradually, yolks and coffee. Slice sponge cake. Arrange slices to cover bottom and sides of a buttered pan. Pour some of the coffee sauce over cake. Place another layer of cake and pour more sauce. Repeat to fill pan. Cover and put some weight on top to press down. Place in refrigerator for several hours. Remove from pan and sprinkle almonds on top.

LARD COOKIES I
100 cookies
Polvorones

3 cups flour	1 beaten yolk
⅛ teaspoon salt	1 beaten white
1 cup sugar	1 tablespoon butter
1 cup lard	

Sift flour and salt. Beat lard to a creamy consistency and add sugar, gradually. Add yolk, white and butter. Add flour and mix well. Take a teaspoonful and shape into ball, place on baking sheet. With the blade of a spatula flatten each ball to a round shape. Bake in moderate oven (350° F) for 10–15minutes.

LARD COOKIES II
40 cookies
Mantecados

2 cups flour	½ cup sugar
½ teaspoon salt	½ cup lard

Mix and sift sugar, flour and salt together. Add flour to fat working with the fingers to get a stiff dough. With floured hands shape the dough into balls. Place on baking sheet and flatten to a round shape. With a knife mark crosswise. Sprinkle with colored sugar. Bake in a moderate oven (350° F) for 10–15 minutes.

RUM COOKIES
50 cookies
Mantecados con Ron

½ pound sugar	¼ pound lard
½ pound flour	⅛ teaspoon salt
2 tablespoons rum	

Sift the sugar, flour and salt together. Add flour to the lard cutting with two knives or working with the fingers. Add the rum and mix well. Shape balls and place in baking sheet. Flatten to a round shape. Bake in hot oven (400° F) for 10–15 minutes.

COCOANUT COOKIES

30 cookies

½ cup butter
½ cup sugar
1 beaten egg
1½ cups flour

1 cup grated cocoanut
1½ teaspoons baking powder
¼ teaspoon salt
⅓ cup milk

Beat butter, add sugar gradually and egg. Sift flour, salt and baking powder together. Add flour and cocoanut to butter alternating with milk. Drop mixture by teaspoonfuls on a greased baking sheet. Bake in hot oven (400° F) for 10 or 15 minutes.

COCOANUT MACAROONS

10 macaroons

Besitos de Coco

1½ cups grated cocoanut
4 tablespoons flour

½ cup sugar
1 teaspoon vanilla

Mix all the ingredients and beat to mix well. Drop by teaspoonfuls on a greased baking sheet. Bake in a moderate oven (350° F) for 20 minutes. Remove from sheet while hot.

COCOANUT BALLS

15–20 balls

1½ cups grated cocoanut
1½ cups sugar

Grated rind of one lemon

Mix all ingredients and cook at low heat. When mixture is almost dry and separates from sides of pan, pour on a greased platter to cool a little. When easy to handle take a spoonful and shape into balls. Roll in granulated sugar and let dry.

NOTE: To make colored balls a few drops of vegetable coloring may be added to mixture before shaping balls.

CUSTARDS

CARAMEL
Caramelo

1 cup sugar   ⅓ cup boiling water

Melt sugar over a low heat. Stir occasionally to prevent burning of sugar; when it has melted to a light brown syrup, add the boiling water and simmer for a short time. Strain.

BAKED CUSTARD   8 servings
Flan

6 eggs	½ teaspoon salt
9 tablespoons sugar	½ teaspoon vanilla
3 cups milk	Caramel

Beat eggs, enough to mix yolks and whites. Add sugar, milk, salt and vanilla. Strain. Pour caramel in the custard cups, to coat sides and bottom. Pour in the custard mixture. Set the cups in a pan with hot water and bake in a moderate oven (350° F) for 1 hour or until firm.

PINEAPPLE CUSTARD   8 servings

2 cups pineapple juice	8 eggs
1 cup sugar	

Boil pineapple juice and sugar to a syrup consistency. Cool. Beat eggs slightly and add pineapple syrup. Strain and bake same as Baked Custard.

ORANGE CUSTARD   8 servings

Follow directions for Pineapple Custard but using orange juice instead of pineapple juice.

COFFEE CUSTARD   6 servings

4 eggs	¼ teaspoon salt
6 tablespoons sugar	⅓ cup coffee extract
2 cups milk	

Beat eggs slightly, add sugar, milk and salt. Strain and add coffee. Bake as Baked Custard.

BOILED CUSTARD   6 servings

2 egg yolks	4 cups hot milk
¾ cup sugar	2 pieces lemon rind
¼ teaspoon salt	Meringue
6 tablespoons cornstarch	2 egg whites
	4 tablespoons sugar

Beat yolks, add sugar, salt and cornstarch. Add milk slowly to yolk mixture, and lemon rind. Cook in double boiler or directly over low heat. When mixture thickens and starch is cooked remove from heat and serve in sauce dishes. Beat egg whites until foamy, add sugar and garnish custard. Instead of meringue, custard may be sprinkled with cinnamon.

CARAMEL CUSTARD   6 servings

Follow directions for Boiled Custard. Serve in a large platter, cover with a thick layer of brown sugar. Use a very hot iron and run lightly over layer of sugar, to melt sugar into caramel. Repeat until all sugar is melted.

FLOATING ISLAND   6 servings
Isla Flotante

Follow recipe for Boiled Custard but use only 3 tablespoons cornstarch to get a soft custard. Pour in sauce dishes or sherbet glasses. Beat the egg whites like meringue, add sugar. Drop by teaspoonfuls over the soft custard to form the "islands".

PUDDINGS

Puddings are desserts easy to prepare. Although the pudding originated in England, it has become an international dish. Each country uses its native foods in new combinations.

In Puerto Rico puddings are usually made from stale bread but crackers and left over cake are also used, they may also be made from cereals, vegetables and fruits. To bread or fruit puddings rum is sometimes poured and light it when serving.

BANANA PUDDING   6–8 servings

4 sliced bananas	2 tablespoons melted butter
3 tablespoons lemon juice	1½ cups milk
1 tablespoon grated lemon rind	3 beaten eggs
½ cup sugar	¾ cup sugar
3 cups bread crumbs	

Cover bottom of a buttered baking pan with ⅓ of the sliced bananas, pour over ⅓ of the lemon juice and sprinkle ⅓ of sugar. Place 1 cup bread crumbs over bananas. Repeat two times more until you have used all the ingredients. Mix butter, sugar, milk and eggs and pour over bread. Place the pudding pan into a larger pan with hot water and bake in a moderate oven for 35 minutes.

BREAD PUDDING   16 servings

½ pound stale bread
4 cups hot milk
4 beaten eggs
1 cup sugar
1 teaspoon cinnamon

4 tablespoons melted butter
¼ teaspoon salt
1 cup raisins
3 tablespoons flour

Remove crust, cut bread in cubes and soak in milk for 5 to 10 minutes. Mix well and strain. Dredge raisins with flour and add to bread mixture. Add the rest of the ingredients. Pour in a buttered or caramel lined baking pan and bake in a moderate oven for 40 to 60 minutes.

PUMPKIN PUDDING   12 to 16 servings
Pudín de Calabaza

3 cups mashed pumpkin
6 tablespoons melted butter
9 tablespoons flour
1 teaspoon salt

1 cup sugar
½ cup milk
1 teaspoon vanilla
5 beaten eggs

Add butter, salt and flour to the pumpkin and mix well. Add the sugar and milk and strain. Add eggs and vanilla and pour in a buttered baking pan. Bake in a moderate oven for 45 minutes.

RICE PUDDING   8 servings

1½ cups cooked rice
¾ cup sugar
¼ teaspoon salt
1 cup milk

¾ cups raisins
2 tablespoons melted butter
2 beaten eggs

Mix all ingredients in the order written. Pour the mixture into a buttered baking pan. Bake in a moderate oven (350° F) for 30 minutes.

[116]

SWEET POTATO PUDDING
Pudín de Batata

8–10 servings

1 pound sweet potato boiled and mashed	¼ cup milk
	2 tablespoons melted butter
½ cup sugar	2 beaten eggs
¼ teaspoon cinnamon	¼ teaspoon salt
¼ cup flour	

Mix all ingredients in the order written. Beat to mix well. Pour in a buttered baking pan and bake in a moderate oven for 20 to 30 minutes.

SWEET POTATO AND ORANGE PUDDING

8–10 servings

1 pound sweet potato boiled and mashed	1 tablespoon grated lemon rind
	½ cup orange juice
3 tablespoons melted butter	¼ teaspoon salt
½ cup brown sugar	

To the mashed sweet potato add all the ingredients and mix well. Pour in a buttered baking dish and bake in a moderate oven for 30 minutes.

FRUIT PUDDING

When Bread Pudding is almost done, cover with a cup of diced fruits. Beat 4 eggs whites until foamy, add 6 tablespoons sugar and ¼ teaspoon cream of tartar. Spread meringue over fruits and place in oven again. Remove from oven when meringue is firm.

SWEET POTATO DESSERTS

Because of the sugar content of sweet potato it is used in combination with other food materials in preparing several popular desserts. The best sweet potato variety is the "mameya" which should be always used when available at the market.

CAZUELA

16 servings

2 cups mashed sweet potato	2 teaspoons cinnamon
2 cups mashed pumpkin	¾ teaspoon cloves
¼ cup rice flour	4 beaten eggs
½ teaspoon salt	1 cup cocoanut milk
¾ cup sugar	2 tablespoons sweet wine

Mix sweet potato and pumpkin, and strain to remove any fiber. Add the other ingredients in the order they are written. Pour mixture in greased pudding pan and bake in a moderate oven (350° F) for 30 minutes or until firm. See illustration.

NÍSPEROS DE BATATA   20 nísperos

1 pound sweet potato   Ground cinnamon
1 pound sugar   Whole cloves

Boil and mash sweet potatoes. Add sugar and cook at low heat until mixture thickens and separates from sides of pan. Pour on shallow pan and let cool. Take about a tablespoonful of the mixture and shape into a ball. To prevent sticking, sprinkle hands with cinnamon. Shape to resemble a "níspero". Tie a knot of green thread or wool around a whole clove and stick to simulate the stem of the "níspero".

SWEET POTATO PASTE   16 servings
Pasta de Batata

4 cups mashed sweet potato   ½ teaspoon almond or vanilla
4 cups sugar   extract

Mix sweet potato and sugar and cook at low heat. When mixture gets thick and separates from sides of pan, remove from heat. Pour on greased pan about ¾ inch thick, and let dry.

SWEET POTATO AND
PINEAPPLE PASTE   16 servings

Follow directions for Sweet Potato Paste and substitute 2 cups of mashed potato for 2 cups grated pineapple.

SWEET POTATO AND   16 servings
COCOANUT PASTE

To Sweet Potato Paste add 1 cup cocoanut milk and 1 cup sugar and follow directions for Sweet Potato Paste.

GALICIAN FRITTERS
Torrejas Gallegas

6 servings

½ pound stale French bread
1 cup milk
½ cup sweet wine
½ teaspoon cinnamon
2 beaten eggs
½ teaspoon salt

Syrup
2 cups sugar
1 cup water
1 stick cinnamon
Fat for frying

Cut bread into ½ inch slices, remove crust. Soak bread in milk and then in wine, and sprinkle with cinnamon. Dip slices in beaten eggs and fry to a golden brown. Drain on paper. Prepare a syrup by boiling water and sugar and cinnamon. Let cool. Pour syrup over fritters.

AIR CRULLERS
Buñuelos de Viento

6 servings

1 cup water
2 tablespoons butter
¼ teaspoon salt
1 teaspoon sugar
¼ teaspoon anise seeds
1 cup flour

4 eggs
Syrup
2 cups sugar
1 cup water
2 sticks cinnamon
Fat for frying

Boil the water with butter, salt, sugar and anise seeds. Add flour at once and stir vigorously until mixture is compact and clings to the spoon. Remove from heat and let cool. Add the eggs one at a time and beat fast a few minutes after each egg is added. Drop by teaspoonfuls and fry in deep fat. When crullers come up to the surface reduce heat and pour hot fat over them. When golden brown and crisp remove and drain on absorbent paper. With sugar and water and cinnamon prepare a syrup. Serve fritters with syrup.

COCADA

8 servings

2 cups of Cocoanut Preserve
2 tablespoons butter

2 beaten eggs
2 ounces chopped almonds

Add butter and eggs to Cocoanut Preserve. Pour in greased pan and place almonds on top. Bake in a moderate oven for 15 to 20 minutes.

MERINGUES
10 meringues

3 egg whites	Peel of 1 lemon
¼ teaspoon cream of tartar	1 cup sugar

Beat whites until stiff. Add sugar slowly, cream of tartar, and lemon peel. Wet a pine board, cover with wet paper also. Drop by spoonfuls, from side of spoon on the paper so mound of mixture has an oval shape. Bake in a moderate oven (325° F) for 15 or 20 minutes until meringues are dry. Remove from paper while hot and put in pairs, so flat bottom will stick together to form the meringues. Let cool. If desired may add few drops of vegetable coloring to get different colors.

JACOB'S STICKS
25 sticks

Palitos de Jacob

1 cup water	Caramel
½ cup butter	½ cup water
1 cup flour	2 cups sugar
4 eggs	Guava jelly

Boil water and butter and add flour at once. Stir constantly to prevent lumps. When mixture clings to the spoon, remove from heat. Add the eggs, one at a time; and beat vigorously after each one. Drop by spoonfuls on a greased baking sheet, with the help of a knife, extend dough to an oblong shape. Bake at a temperature of 375° F for 45 minutes. Remove from oven and let cool. Split and fill each stick with guava jelly. Prepare caramel with water and sugar and pour over each stick.

ROYAL YOLKS
8 servings

Yemas Reales

7 yolks	Syrup
2 whites	2 cups sugar
2 tablespoons cornstarch	1 cup water
1 teaspoon baking powder	1 stick cinnamon

Beat yolks until thick. Beat whites until foamy and fold into the yolk mixture. Mix cornstarch and baking powder and fold into egg mixture carefully and thoroughly. Grease a shallow pan and pour in mixture. Bake in a moderate oven (350° F), for 30 minutes. Remove from pan and cut into 1¼″ squares. Boil sugar, water and cinnamon; when syrup begins to thicken add few squares ("yemas") at a time and cook for 2 minutes or until they have absorbed some syrup. Remove, place "yemas" in serving dish and pour over remaining syrup.

RICE WITH COCOANUT   8 servings
Arroz con Coco

1 cup rice	6 cinnamon sticks
1 cocoanut	1 teaspoon whole cloves
1 cup sugar	½ cup raisins
1 teaspoon salt	Ground cinnamon
1 piece chopped ginger	

Place rice in water for two hours. Grate cocoanut and add about 5 cups hot water to get 6 cups cocoanut milk. Add ginger, cloves, cinnamon sticks, salt and rice to 5 cups cocoanut milk and cook at low heat. When rice is tender and almost dry, add 1 cup cocoanut milk, sugar and raisins. Stir well and continue cooking over very low heat. When rice is almost dry remove from heat. Pour in a platter and sprinkle with cinnamon. See illustration.

SWEET RICE   12 servings
Arroz con Dulce

6 cups water	4 tablespoons lard
1 piece chopped ginger	1 tablespoon salt
½ teaspoon anise seeds	1 tablespoon ground anise seeds
1¼ cups rice	1 tablespoon ground cinnamon
1 cup sugar	1 teaspoon ground cloves
1 ground cassava cake	

Place rice in water for two hours. Boil water with ginger and anise seeds and strain. Cook rice in ginger water at low heat. When rice is tender add sugar, lard and salt, and continue cooking. Before removing from heat add the ground anise seeds, cinnamon and cloves. Pour in serving dish and sprinkle with ground cassava cake.

RICE WITH MILK   10 servings

1 cup rice   1 stick cinnamon
4 cups milk   1 cup sugar
1 teaspoon salt

Place rice in water for two hours. Remove from water and drain. Add
milk, salt and cinnamon and cook at low heat, stirring constantly.
When rice is tender and almost dry, add sugar. Stir well and cook for
few minutes. Remove from heat and serve.

MAZAMORRA   8 servings

12 corn ears[1]   1 teaspoon salt
1 quart milk   Ground cinnamon
½ cup sugar

Grate corn, add the milk and strain through a very fine sieve or cheese
cloth. Add sugar and salt. Cook at low heat stirring constantly until
mixture thickens. Pour in dishes and sprinkle with cinnamon.

TEMBLEQUE   6 servings

1 grated cocoanut   ½ cup cornstarch
Hot water   ¼ teaspoon salt
½ cup sugar   Ground cinnamon

Add hot water to the cocoanut. Place in cheese cloth bag and squeeze
to extract 4 cups milk. Mix cornstarch and salt. Add the cocoanut
milk and cook at low heat, stirring constantly. When starch grains
are cooked and mixture thickens remove from heat. Pour in wet cups
or dishes and let cool. Sprinkle with cinnamon.

MAJARETE   6 servings

6 tablespoons rice meal   2 cups hot milk
¾ teaspoon salt   1 piece lemon rind
5 tablespoons sugar   Ground cinnamon

Mix rice meal, salt and sugar. Add milk and lemon rind. Cook at low
heat, stirring constantly to prevent lumps. When mixture thickens
pour in dishes. Let cool and sprinkle with cinnmon.

---

[1] Choose sweet corn, just beginning to get dry, or "sarazo" which is a stage
between fresh and dry corn.

ALFAJOR
8 alfajores

1 cup ground cassava
2 cups brown sugar
1 cup water

1 piece chopped ginger
¼ cup ground cassava

Mix 1 cup ground cassava, sugar, water and ginger. Cook at low heat until mixture separates from sides of pan. Remove the ginger and pour mixture in a pan to a thickness of about 1½ inch. Mark in squares, and sprinkle with ground cassava.

MAMPOSTIAL O MARRAYO
12 servings

1½ cups molasses

1½ cups grated cocoanut

Mix and cook at low heat. When mixture gets thick and separates from sides of pan, remove from heat. Pour on a buttered platter and mark in squares. Cut and serve.

CANDIES

TIRIJALA O MELCOCHA
6 pieces
Molasses Taffy

Boil 2 cups of molasses. When the syrup becomes thick, remove from heat. Pour about ¼ teaspoon of the hot syrup in a sauce dish nearly full of cold water, if it forms a soft ball when shaped with the fingers, pour the syrup in a buttered shallow dish. When it gets lukewarm remove from dish and begin to pull, or stretch. Do this fast and as soon as it gets a light golden color and begins to harden, pull a long strip about ¾ of an inch thick and 1 inch wide, mark with blunt edge of knife. Cut in pieces when cold.

TURRON DE COCO
12 pieces
Cocoanut Taffy

2 cups sugar
¼ teaspoon cream of tartar

⅔ cup cocoanut milk
1 teaspoon vinegar

Mix sugar, cream of tartar, milk and vinegar. Cook without stirring. Clean the sides of the pan with a wet piece of cloth wrapped in the tines of a fork. When syrup becomes thick and dense remove from heat and follow directions as for Tirijala. Pull to strips about 1 inch wide, mark and cut in pieces.

ALFEÑIQUE

12 alfeñiques

2 cups sugar
¼ teaspoon cream of tartar
⅔ cup water

1 teaspoon vinegar
¼ teaspoon oil of peppermint

Mix sugar, cream of tartar, water and vinegar. Follow directions for Tirijala. When lukewarm and before pulling, add oil of peppermint. Pull and shape in a roll about ½ inch in diameter. Mark and cut in strips about 4 inches long.

For Fruit Preserves and Fruit Ices, please see Chapter III.

CHAPTER XI

MENUS

The following sample menus will help the reader to use the recipes given in this book.

One-dish meals

Chicken Asopao
Tomato and Lettuce Salad
Papaya Preserve
Coffee or Milk

Sancocho
Bread
Baked Custard
Coffee or Milk

Pigs' Feet Stew
Bread
Fruit Cocktail
Coffee or Milk

Galician Broth
Mixed Vegetable Salad
Bread
Royal Yolks
Milk or Coffee

Cocido   Boiled Rice
Tomato Salad
Floating Island   Milk or Coffee

Piñón   Boiled Yam
Cabbage Salad   Bread
Lemon Ice

During lent fish and eggs dishes are most popular and among them are the "cocas" or Sardine Pies, Codfish, Biscayan Style, Pickled Fish and Buche de Bacalao Stew, omelets and eggs dishes.

Grapefruit
Potato Omelet
Baked Pepper and Tomato Salad
Bread
Cocada   Milk or Coffee

Pickled Fish   Mashed Yautía
Cucumber Salad   Bread
Guava Shells Preserve
Milk or Coffee

Sardine Pie
Chayote Salad   Bread
Boiled Custard
Milk or Coffee

Codfish, Biscayan Style
Boiled Green Bananas and Sweet Potato
Lettuce Salad
Cherry Ice
Milk or Coffee

Buche de Bacalao Stew
Baked Amarillos
Baked Pepper Salad   Bread
Gypsy's Arm
Milk or Coffee

Eggs, Flemish Style   Glazed Sweet Potato
Water Cress and Chayote Salad
Spice Cake   Milk or Coffee

[126]

Beefsteak Fried Potatoes
Boiled Rice Bean Stew
String Beans Salad
Guava Paste Milk or Coffee

Vermicelli Soup
Larded Meat and Potatoes
Stewed Rice and Beans
Lettuce Salad Sour Orange Paste
Milk or Coffee

Rice, Garden Style Bean Stew
Scrambled Eggs with Codfish
Cucumber Salad Fruit Cocktail
Milk or Coffee

Rice and Okra Fresh Navy Bean Stew
Pork Turnovers Tomato Salad
Fresh Pineapple Coffee

Chicken and Rice Bean Stew
Ripe Plantain in Syrup
Lettuce and Chayote Salad
Meringue Milk
Coffee

Boiled Rice
Pigeon Peas with Plantain Balls
Stuffed Pepper Tomato Salad
Cocoanut Preserve
Milk or Coffee

The Christmas Eve Supper or "Cena de Nochebuena" is served at midnight or after mass (misa de gallo). This is an occasion for family reunion and gay parties.

Christmas Punch
Pasteles   Chicken and Rice
Red Wine
String Beans and Tomato Salad
Sour Orange Preserve   Native Cheese

Raisins   Nuts   Majarete
Coffee

Rum Punch
Hayacas   Rice Meal Cruller
Rice and Pork Meat
Water Cress Salad
Raisins   Nougat   Bienmesabe
Anis   Coffee

Stuffed Olives   Pickles
Boiled Ham in Wine
Rice Meal Cruller   Lettuce and Tomato Salad
Rice with Cocoanut
Pound Cake   Nuts   Raisins
Creme de Cacao   Coffee

Christmas Eggnog
Gandinga   Tostones
Stewed Rice and Pigeon Peas
Egg and Potato Salad   Nougat
Nuts   Raisins   Coffee

Christmas Day or New Year Menus

Fruit Cocktail
Sour Sweet Hen   Breadfruit Chips
Fried Eggplant   Bread
Cucumber Salad
Spice Cake   Lemon Ice
Nuts   Almond Nougat
Coffee

Rum Eggnog
Roast Pig   Baked Plantain
Gandinga   Boiled Rice
Lettuce Salad
Tipsy Cake   Nuts   Nougat
Coffee

Christmas Punch
Stuffed Turkey   Mashed Potato
Buttered Peas   Platanutri
Stuffed Tomato Salad
Pumpkin Pudding   Nuts   Coffee

Olives   Salami
Chicken Pie
Rice and Native Sausage   Bean Stew
Lettuce Salad
Cocada   Native Cheese   Nuts   Raisins
Coffee

Three Kings' Day Menus

The "Trulla" is the traditional party of Three Kings' Day. A group of people meet and singing the "villancicos" or Christmas songs, start a round of visits to different homes, where they stop to

[129]

sing and have a good time; of course, they expect to be treated with the foods typical of the season.

Anis

Pork Turnovers   Bacalaitos
Rum Punch   Dates
Majarete
Coffee

Sangría
Pasteles   Rice Meal Cruller
Figs   Alfajor
Coffee

Rum Punch
Roast Pig   Tostones
Stewed Rice and Pigeon Peas
Sour Orange Preserve   Coffee

Hayacas   Bread
Spanish Red Wine
Majarete   Figs   Nuts
Coffee   Mabi   Nougat

Gandinga   Boiled Rice
Alcapurrias
Nougat   Raisins
Cazuela   Coffee

Morcilla[1]   Chicharrones
Surullitos
Rice with Cocoanut
Papaya Preserve   Native Cheese
Coffee   Rum Punch

[1] Blood sausage.

Cassava Soup
Rabbit with Sherry   Boiled Rice
Cucumber and Avocado Salad
Bread
Tembleque
Coffee or Milk

Fruit Cocktail
Baked Fresh Ham
Tostones   Glazed Sweet Potatoes
String Bean Salad
Native Cherry Ice   Polvorones
Coffee or Milk

Plantain Soup
Stuffed Pepper
Rice and Link Sausage
Chick Peas Stew
Lettuce Salad   Bread
Guava Paste   Native Cheese
Coffee or Milk

Vermicelli Soup
Canelones
Ripe Plantain in Syrup
Eggs and String Beans Salad
Orange Ice
Coffee or Milk

Plantain Balls Soup
Stuffed Cheese with Spaghetti
Tomato Salad   Bread
Gypsy's Arm
Coffee or Milk

Yautía Soup
Pizza with Mozzarella   Chianti Wine
Mashed Breadfruit
Chayote Salad
Guava Shells Preserve
Coffee or Milk

[131]

OTHER RECIPES

The recipes for Majorca Rolls and Sardine Pie are quite typical and should not be left out of this book; the recipes for pizzas, while not a Puerto Rican dish are becoming very popular.

SARDINE PIE   6 servings
Coca de Sardinas

Pie Shell

1 package active dry yeast	3 tablespoons melted butter
½ cup lukewarm water	1 beaten egg
1 teaspoon sugar	2 cups flour
½ teaspoon salt	

Add 1 teaspoon sugar to the lukewarm water, then add the yeast slowly and let stand for 10 minutes. Add the salt, butter, and egg and mix well. Add the flour slowly to form a smooth dough. Knead lightly and place in a greased bowl. Let rise until double in bulk. Take half of the dough and roll into a circle, about 10 inches in diameter and ¼ inch thick. Place dough in a 9 inch pie tin and build up the extra 1 inch edge to form a ridge.

Filling

1 bunch swiss chard	1 tablespoon salt
½ pound chopped tomatoes	¼ cup olive oil
½ pound chopped onions	2 pimentos cut into strips
¼ pound chopped green pep-	10 sardines
per	

Cut chard into 1″ pieces, add vegetables and sauté in olive oil. Pour into pie shell and spread on bottom. Place sardines on top, spreading out like sun rays. Place strips of pimento on the sardines and between them. Bake in a moderate oven, 350° F for 25 minutes.

MAJORCA ROLLS   12 rolls
Pan de Mallorca

1 package active dry yeast	1 teaspoon sugar
1 cup lukewarm water	1 cup flour

Add sugar to the lukewarm water and mix, then add yeast and let stand for 10 minutes or until double in bulk. Beat and add the flour, mix well, cover with a towel and let rise in a warm place until double in bulk. Then add the following:

¼ cup sugar	4 tablespoons olive oil
4 beaten eggs	2 cups flour
½ teaspoon salt	

Mix thoroughly and let stand for 4 or 5 hours. Then add the following:

½ cup sugar	2 teaspoons salt
½ cup olive oil	4 to 5 cups flour

Rub the bread board with oil and knead dough until smooth. Place dough in a greased bowl and allow to stand until double in bulk. Divide dough into 12 portions. Roll each portion into a very thin oblong about 12 inches long and 3 inches wide. Roll lengthwise and finally holding one end roll around in circles. The loose end should be pressed under so it will keep the shape. Place in a baking sheet and let stand for about 6 or 8 hours. Bake in a moderately hot oven for 15 to 20 minutes. As soon as removed from the baking sheet sprinkle each roll with powdered sugar.

Suggested time table for preparing Majorca Rolls:

AM	8:00–9:00	Start
	11:00–12:00	Add eggs and other ingredients
PM	5:00–6:00	Combine remaining flour and knead.
	10:00–11:00	Shape rolls and let stand over night.
AM	6:00–7:00	Bake (Next day)

Making Majorca Rolls is a 24 hours job, but it is worth the trouble.

PIZZA DOUGH 2–12″ pizzas

1 package active dry yeast	4 tablespoons sugar
½ cup lukewarm water	¾ cup hot water
1 teaspoon sugar	1 beaten egg
6 tablespoons lard	5 cups flour
1 teaspoon salt	

Add 1 teaspoon sugar to the lukewarm water and stir to dissolve sugar. Sprinkle the yeast and let stand for 10 minutes. Mix and add beaten egg and beat again. To the hot water add the lard, salt and sugar. When lukewarm mix with yeast. Beat and add enough flour to make a soft dough. Place dough in a greased bowl, cover with a towel and let rise in a warm place for 1 hour, or until double in bulk. Knead on a floured board and divide into two pieces. Roll lightly and stretch each piece on the bottom of a greased 12 inch pizza plate.

PIZZA WITH SAUSAGE
6–8 servings

½ pound Spanish sausages
2 tablespoons olive oil
1 no. 2 can tomatoes, drained
½ teaspoon salt

¼ teaspoon pepper
½ teaspoon sugar
½ pound sliced mozzarella cheese

Cut sausages into thin slices. Heat oil, add tomatoes, salt, pepper and sugar. Boil and mash tomatoes as they are over the heat. Stretch dough over pizza plate and pour first the tomato sauce, then the sliced sausages and sliced cheese. Bake in a hot oven 400°F for 15 or 20 minutes.

PIZZA WITH ANCHOVIES
6 to 8 servings

1 recipe Pizza Dough
1 no. 2 can tomatoes, drained
18 anchovy filets
¼ teaspoon salt

½ teaspoon pepper
3 tablespoons olive oil
1 teaspoon orégano

Stretch dough over 2 12 inch pizza plates. Spread tomatoes over dough. Place anchovies over tomatoes, sprinkle with salt, pepper, olive oil and orégano and bake in hot oven (400°F) 20 minutes, or until edges of dough are crisp.

PIZZA WITH MOZZARELLA
6–8 servings

1 recipe Pizza Dough
1 no. 2 can tomatoes, drained
½ teaspoon salt
½ teaspoon freshly ground pepper

¾ pound mozzarella cheese sliced thin
3 tablespoons olive oil
1 teaspoon orégano (optional)

Spread out dough over bottoms of two 12 inch pizza plates. Arrange half the tomatoes over dough in each plate, sprinkle with salt and pepper and arrange mozzarella slices over tomatoes. Sprinkle with olive oil and orégano and bake in hot oven (400°F) 20 minutes, or until cheese is melted and edges of dough are crisp.

Roast Pig
(Lechón Asado)

Roast pig is the traditional dish for the Christmas festivities, picnics and other outdoor entertainments.

A suckling pig, three or four months old, with an average weight of 30 pounds, will yield about 15 pounds of roast meat. There is much waste due to losses in dressing and during roasting. An estimate of one or two pounds of the live pig is considered an adequate portion. When the pig is slaughtered the blood is collected for preparing blood sausage. The internal organs are removed carefully: liver, heart, lungs and kidneys, to be used in a stew "gandinga". Sections of the intestines are saved for the blood sausage. They are cleaned and washed with sour orange or lemon juice.

For a home party the pig can be baked at home. The baking pan should have a rack, so fat will drip. The temperature is 325°, and for a pig weighing about 25 pounds, the roasting time is from four to five hours. For outside parties, the pig is roasted on the spot, adding more interest to the entertainment. When the pig is cleaned, the belly is opened in the center, leaving an opening only large enough to remove the internal organs. After the pig is dressed a pole is passed through the body. The pig is roasted on an open fire of live charcoal, placed over a layer of stones. The stones will get hot and keep a constant temperature. At both sides of the fire two forked poles are driven into the ground to hold the pole with the pig over the fire. The pole is turned slowly all the time and the pig is basted with achote coloring so it will roast and brown evenly. Roasting time is from four to six hours, according to size of pig.

ROAST PIG   15 to 20 servings
Lechón Asado

1–30 pounds suckling pig, ready to cook	½ cup salt
2 whole bulbs garlic	4 tablespoons marjoran
	2 tablespoons pepper

Mix salt, pepper, garlic and marjoran and chop together thoroughly. Make deep gashes in shoulder, loin, legs, hips, under legs, in jowl and neck and also inside the body. Then rub generously with dressing. Place in refrigerator over night, as it is better to dress the pig several hours previous to roasting. Place pig in baking pan with rack. Bake in a moderate hot oven 325° for about 5 hours. While baking, baste occasionally with fat drippings. Serve with baked green plantain and ajilimójili. See illustration.

BLOOD SAUSAGE
(Morcilla)

8 servings

2 tablespoons diced cilantro
2 chopped sweet peppers
3 chopped hót peppers
1½ tablespoons salt

2½ cups blood
¾ cup fat from intestines
1 yard pork intestines

Remove some of the fat that is found surrounding the intestines of the pork. Cut the fat in small pieces. Stir blood to cut clots. Add seasoning ingredients and mix thoroughly. Wash the pork intestines carefully turning them inside out so that they will be clean. Rinse with water mixed with sour orange or lemon juice. Tie one end of the intestine and stuff, using a funnel. The sausage filling should be somewhat loose. Tie the other end and cook in boiling salted water for 25 minutes. When done the sausage should be firm. Drain and keep in refrigerator and fry for a few minutes before serving. Drain.

GLOSSARY

Agualoja	Cold drink made with ginger, cinnamon and molasses; anise seeds may be added, the name is derived from "aloja" a 17th century cold drink made in Spain with honey and spices.
Ajilimójili	Piquant sauce made with hot peppers and garlic to serve with pork, roast pig and other meats.
Ajonjolí	Sesame seed. The seed of a herbaceous plant, rich in oil of fine quality; the seed is used for "horchatas" and "dulces".
Alboronía	Stew made with chayote and eggs.
Alfajor	Some kind of pudding which has ground cassava, ginger, brown sugar or molasses.
Alfeñique	Stick candy.
Almojábanas	Fritter made from rice flour with native cheese and leavened with plenty of eggs.
Amarillo	Ripe plantain.
Achote	Red seeds rich in vitamin A. The coloring material is extracted when seeds are cooked in fat; it is used to color rice, soup and other dishes.
Arepitas	Flat, round fritters made of cornmeal and native cheese.
Asopao	Rice with chicken having the consistency of a thick soup.
Bienmesabe	A dessert; sponge cake with a cocanut milk and egg sauce poured over it.
Buche de bacalao	The dried lining of the stomach of the codfish.
Butifarra	Link sausage made of pork, seasoned with nutmeg and pepper.
Caldero	Pot made of iron or cast aluminum; has a round bottom and straight sides with two small handles (asas).
Canelones	Large, round macaroni. From the Italian "cannelloni", meaning "big pipe".
Caramelo	Burnt sugar syrup.
Casabe	Flat, round, dry cake made from grated yuca.

Cazuela	Pudding made with sweet potato, pumpkin, cocoanut milk, spices, etc.
Cocada	A dessert made by adding butter and eggs to cocoanut preserve.
Cocido	Spanish stew or thick soup made with chick peas, meat and vegetables. A one dish meal.
Chicharrones	Pork skin, salted and fried to remove all fat so that it is hard and crusty.
Chorizo	Spanish sausage, made of pork and smoked.
Dulce	(Preserve). Any fruit cooked in water with sugar. The fruit gets soft and the syrup heavy, called "almíbar" ex. "dulce de coco" or "dulce de papaya" or "dulces en almíbar".
Empanada	A meat pie, the dough is made of a grated vegetable such as yuca and a pork filling.
Empanada, carne	Breaded meat.
Escabeche	Any meat or fish pickled in a sauce made with oil, vinegar, pepper, bay leaves and onions.
Flan	A custard, baked in a cup lined with caramel.
Frituras	Name given to a group of fried foods, such as crullers, fritters, etc.
Gandinga	The heart, kidney, liver and lungs of pork cut up into small pieces and cooked.
Gazpacho	Cold soup; main ingredients are: olive oil, vinegar, bread and chopped vegetables.
Gragea	Minute confit. Used to decorate "sopa borracha" and other desserts.
Guanimes	Boiled pie made of cornmeal, cocoanut milk, sugar and other ingredients.
Hayacas	Boiled pie; the dough or "masa" is made of green corn or pearl hominy and stuffed with a meat filling.
Hojaldre	A spice cake with wine.
Horchata	A cold drink made from sesame seed or almond. Seed is pounded or ground to extract the "milk", which is mixed with water and sugar.
Lechón	Cut obtained from the round; is long and round like a large sausage. Called "lechón"

	because its shape resembles that of a small pig.
Longaniza	A pork sausage seasoned with salt, garlic, pepper, orégano and achote coloring.
Mabí	Fermented beverage made with water, sugar and the bark of the mabí tree (colurina reclinata).
Majarete	Dessert made of rice meal and milk.
Mantecado	A lard cookie; also means French ice cream.
Marrayo o mampostial	Dessert made of grated cocoanut and molasses.
Mazamorra	Grated green corn, milk and sugar and cinnamon made into a delicious dessert.
Mofongo	Fried "tostones" then ground and mixed with ground "chicharrones" shaped into balls.
Mondongo	Lining of the calf or pork's stomach; tripe.
Morcilla	Sausage made from pork blood and seasoned.
Níspero de batata	Sweet potato paste, shaped into balls to resemble the fruit "níspero".
Native cheese	A cheese made at Arecibo, it has a smooth texture, mild flavor, called "Queso de Crema".
Paella	Spanish dish containing rice, meat, and vegetables, very popular in the Valencia region.
Pastel	The dough or "masa" is prepared by grating plantain or yautía and plantain or green bananas. Prepared with a meat filling the same as the hayaca.
Pastelillos	Fried turnover; may be made with a meat or cheese filling or guava paste.
Pastelón	A meat, fish or poultry pie.
Pilón	(Mortero). A round wooden utensil with a base (resembles the shape of a goblet) and a cavity to pound or chop food with a pestle.
Piñón	A pie made with slices of ripe plantain, string beans, a meat filling and eggs.
Piononos	Slices of ripe plantain shaped into a circle with a meat filling and then fried.
Polvorones	A lard cookie.
Pollo	Young chicken.

Ponqué	A butter cake; the word ponqué is a corruption of the English words "pound cake".
Rancho	A one dish meal prepared for a large group of persons, usually contains meat, vegetables, vermicelli.
Ravioli	A paste rolled into thin squares then stuffed with a meat or chicken or brain and cheese filling. It is cooked and served with a sauce.
Relleno	Stuffed; stuffed vegetables; stuffed turkey (pavo relleno).
Sancocho	A kind of thick soup with vegetables and meat cut into small pieces. A one dish meal.
Serenata	A dish consisting of boiled codfish, served with boiled vegetables and garnished with sliced tomato, onion and eggs.
Sofrito	A mixture of chopped onion, tomato, pepper, ham and bacon and fried; used as a seasoning for many dishes.
Sopa Borracha	"Drunken soup" a tipsy cake, with a wine syrup and covered with meringue and decorated with comfits.
Sopón	A thick soup.
Surullitos	Cylindrical shape fritters made of cornmeal and cheese.
Tembleque	Pudding made with cornstarch and cocoanut milk.
Tirijala	Some kind of taffy candy made with molasses.
Tostones	Slices of plantain, fried slightly, then pressed down to flatten and fried again to a golden color.
Turrón de coco	Candy prepared with sugar and cocoanut milk, has the consistency of a cream candy.

INDEX

[142]